WONDERFUL WORLD OF KNOWLEDGE

YEAR BOOK 1983

Disney's

Wonderful World of Knowledge

YEAR BOOK 1983

GROLIER ENTERPRISES, INC.
Danbury, Connecticut

ROBERT B. CLARKE *Publisher*

WILLIAM E. SHAPIRO   *Editor in Chief*

FERN L. MAMBERG   *Executive Editor*

MICHÈLE A. MCLEAN   *Art Director*

RICHARD SHAW
ALAN PHELPS   *Production Managers*

ISBN 0-7172-8168-X
The Library of Congress Catalog Card Number: 78-66149

CONTENTS

1982 AT A GLANCE

JANUARY 31. January was a month of extreme weather conditions. It was the coldest January in the United States in 100 years. Almost the whole country, including every Southern state, experienced freezing temperatures and snow. The West was hit by high winds, and California was lashed by torrential rains.

FEBRUARY 3. The Eastman Kodak Company introduced a new type of camera that uses a film disk instead of roll film. Kodak said the new system should improve the quality of amateur photography. ■ It was announced that fossils of what may have been the first leaf-eating mammal on Earth had been found in Wyoming. The fossils are of a previously unknown, chipmunklike creature that lived about 130,000,000 years ago. The mammal may have played an important role in the spread of flowers around the world. As it ate flower leaves, it scattered the flower seeds over the Earth.

MARCH 14. It was announced that the jeweled rabbit of Kit Williams' book *Masquerade* had been found. Williams had made the golden rabbit, adorned with precious stones, and buried it in a secret spot in Britain. Clues to its location were given in the book, an illustrated fairy tale published in 1980. The man who found the jeweled rabbit wished to remain anonymous and was given the pseudonym Ken Thomas. He had spent 18 months trying to solve the book's clues. In the end, luck as well as logic led him to the buried treasure, in Ampthill, a village northwest of London.

MARCH 30. Astronauts Jack Lousma and C. Gordon Fullerton ended an eight-day mission aboard the space shuttle *Columbia*. It was the third mission of the re-usable shuttle. The astronauts gathered scientific information and tested the robot arm that would be used to place satellites in orbit.

APRIL 2. Argentine troops invaded the British-ruled Falkland Islands, which lie off the southeastern tip of Argentina. The islands had been under British rule since 1833. But sovereignty over the islands had long been a subject of conflict between Britain and Argentina. Immediately after the invasion, Britain severed diplomatic ties with Argentina. (On April 5, Britain launched a naval task force on the 8,000-mile [13,000-kilometer] voyage to the Falklands. On May 1, serious fighting began.)

APRIL 17. In a historic ceremony in Ottawa, Canada, Queen Elizabeth II of Britain proclaimed the Constitution Act, 1982. This completed the transfer of constitutional powers from Britain to Canada, giving Canada control over its own Constitution and complete legal independence from Britain.

APRIL 25. Israel completed its withdrawal from the Sinai Peninsula. Egypt had lost the Sinai to Israel in 1967, during a war between Israel and the Arab nations. In 1979, Israel and Egypt signed a peace treaty that called for Israel to withdraw from the Sinai in stages over a three-year period.

MAY 1. The 1982 World's Fair in Knoxville, Tennessee, opened. The theme of the fair was "Energy Turns the World." Most of the countries, states, and corporations that had pavilions at the fair devoted their exhibitions to energy—how to obtain it, conserve it, and use it.

MAY 30. Spain became the 16th member of the North Atlantic Treaty Organization (NATO). The other member nations are Belgium, Britain, Canada, Denmark, France, Greece, Iceland, Italy, Luxembourg, the Netherlands, Norway, Portugal, Turkey, West Germany, and the United States.

JUNE 6. Israeli troops invaded Lebanon. The attack was aimed at destroying military bases of the Palestine Liberation Organization (PLO). (By June 10, Israeli troops had reached Beirut, the capital of Lebanon. The city suffered heavy damage, and many civilians were killed. In addition to fighting the PLO, the Israelis were fighting Syrian troops stationed in Lebanon.)

JUNE 14. A cease-fire went into effect on the Falkland Islands. The ten-week-long war ended when Argentine troops surrendered to British forces.

JUNE 21.   Diana, Princess of Wales, gave birth to her first child, a boy. He was named William Arthur Philip Louis, and he will be known as Prince William of Wales. The baby is second in line to the British throne, after his father, Charles, Prince of Wales. ■ A jury found John W. Hinckley, Jr., the man who shot President Ronald Reagan and three other people on March 30, 1981, not guilty by reason of insanity. Hinckley was committed to a mental hospital for an indefinite period of time.

JUNE 25.   Alexander M. Haig, Jr., resigned as U.S. Secretary of State. George P. Shultz was named to succeed Haig.

JUNE 30.   The proposed Equal Rights Amendment (ERA) was defeated when the ratification deadline passed. The amendment, proposed by Congress in 1972, would have provided for equal legal rights for women and men. The amendment had been approved by 35 states, three short of the 38 required for ratification.

JULY 4.   Astronauts Thomas Mattingly 2nd and Henry Hartsfield, Jr., ended a seven-day mission aboard the space shuttle *Columbia*. It was the fourth and final test flight of the spacecraft.

AUGUST 18.   The Lebanese Government and the Palestine Liberation Organization (PLO) approved a plan for the evacuation of Palestinian and Syrian fighters trapped since June in West Beirut by Israeli forces. (On August 19, Israel also approved the plan. The evacuation began on August 21 and was completed on September 1. The PLO guerrillas traveled to various Arab nations. The largest number went to Syria, along with the evacuated Syrian troops. The evacuation was supervised by troops from France, Italy, and the United States.)

SEPTEMBER 4.   At a zoo in Madrid, Spain, a giant panda named Shao Shao gave birth to twin cubs. This was the first time that panda twins had been born in captivity outside of China. One of the two cubs died three days later. The other cub developed normally, receiving lots of attention from its mother.

SEPTEMBER 16–18. Hundreds of Palestinian civilians were massacred by Lebanese Christian militia at refugee camps in West Beirut. On the night of the 16th, Israeli troops, who had been in control of the area, permitted the Lebanese soldiers to move into the camps. The massacre resulted in demands for Israeli withdrawal from West Beirut and for an investigation into the circumstances surrounding the killings.

NOVEMBER 2. In U.S. elections, the Democrats increased their majorities in the House of Representatives and in state governorships. The Republicans retained their majority in the Senate. The breakdown was as follows: The House—267 Democrats, 166 Republicans. The Senate—54 Republicans, 46 Democrats. Governorships—34 Democrats, 16 Republicans. (Elections in Georgia on November 30 gave the Democrats two more House seats.)

NOVEMBER 10. Soviet leader Leonid Brezhnev died at the age of 75. Brezhnev was general secretary of the Communist Party's Central Committee for eighteen years. This is the most important position in the country. (On November 12, Yuri Andropov, 68, was chosen to succeed Brezhnev.)

NOVEMBER 16. Astronauts Vance Brand, Robert Overmyer, William Lenoir, and Joseph Allen ended a five-day mission aboard the space shuttle *Columbia*. But it was not another test flight. This time, the re-usable spacecraft performed the task it was designed to do—deliver satellites into space. It launched two communications satellites into orbit for commercial customers.

DECEMBER 2. Barney Clark, a 61-year-old retired dentist, became the first person to receive a permanent artificial heart. In an operation at the University of Utah Medical Center in Salt Lake City, doctors replaced Clark's dying heart with an artificial heart made of plastic. The plastic device was named Jarvik-7 after its creator, Dr. Robert Jarvik. The artificial heart was slightly larger than a human heart but weighed about the same. It was connected by hoses to its power supply—an external air compressor that was carried in a large cart.

DECEMBER 8. Donald P. Hodel became U.S. Secretary of Energy, succeeding James B. Edwards.

DECEMBER 10. Soviet cosmonauts Anatoly Berezovoy and Valentin Lebedev returned safely to Earth after the longest spaceflight in history. Aboard the Salyut 7 space station for 211 days, they set a new record for the length of time spent in space. The previous record of 185 days had been set in 1980 by two of their countrymen.

BACKYARD WILDLIFE

You don't have to go to a zoo or to distant lands to see animals in the wild. You can find a variety of wildlife right near your home. And with a little bit of effort, you can improve the living conditions for animals and bring that wildlife into your backyard. You can develop a wildlife refuge—an environment that animals will treat as their home. You may attract birds such as robins and orioles, mammals such as rabbits and flying squirrels, and reptiles such as grass snakes and turtles. If there is water near your home, you may see frogs and fish. And everywhere, you will spot butterflies, spiders, and other small creatures.

You don't need a lot of land to develop a wildlife refuge. Even a tiny backyard can be transformed into one. The refuge will do more than help wildlife. It will add beauty and excitement to the land, thereby making it a more delightful place for people as well as animals.

WHAT DO ANIMALS NEED?

Animals look for four things: food, water, hiding places, and nesting places. Each kind of animal has its own needs. What attracts a hummingbird won't interest a robin or a squirrel. Hummingbirds feed on nectar and on the insects that haunt the throats of flowers. They will be attracted by petunias, weigela, and wisteria. Robins eat earthworms and ground insects. You need moist, rich soil to attract them. Squirrels eat acorns. They won't visit you if all you offer are petunias and soil. But if you have a tall oak tree, you'll see squirrels racing up and down its trunk.

Food. Like people, most animals must eat all year round. So it is important that a wildlife refuge provide food throughout the year. Some plants flower in early spring, others flower in summer, still others flower in autumn. All types should be part of your garden. Similarly, different plants produce fruit at different times of the year. Trees such as mountain ash, hawthorn, and autumn olive bear fruit from early autumn until February or March. Thus they make food available during the cold winter months—the time of year when food is scarcest.

You can supplement vegetation with birdseed, suet, bread, corn, raisins, table scraps—you name it. Almost any food found in your kitchen will be welcomed by some creature in your refuge.

But remember that each animal has specific food needs. And like people, it also has favorite foods. If you provide an animal's favorite foods, you will increase the chances of attracting the animal to your garden.

A robin would rather eat an earthworm than a beetle. A purple finch will choose the catkins of bigtooth aspens over the seeds of weeds.

To attract moths and other insects that are active at night, make a sugar bait. A mixture of sugar and stale beer will work. Or mix very ripe bananas with sugar and let the mixture ferment for a day or two. At dusk, paint the sugar bait on tree trunks. Later, after it is dark, use a flashlight to learn who has come to dine.

If you want to attract orioles, provide jelly water. This is a mixture of half water and half grape jelly. Place the mixture in small straight-sided jars. Put the containers on a hanging bird feeder. (Clean the containers occasionally to prevent disease problems.)

There are many types of feeders, each attractive to certain kinds of animals. Some are elaborate structures, others are very simple. In fact, a little imagination can turn almost anything into a feeder. A picnic table can be used as a winter bird feeder. Put the

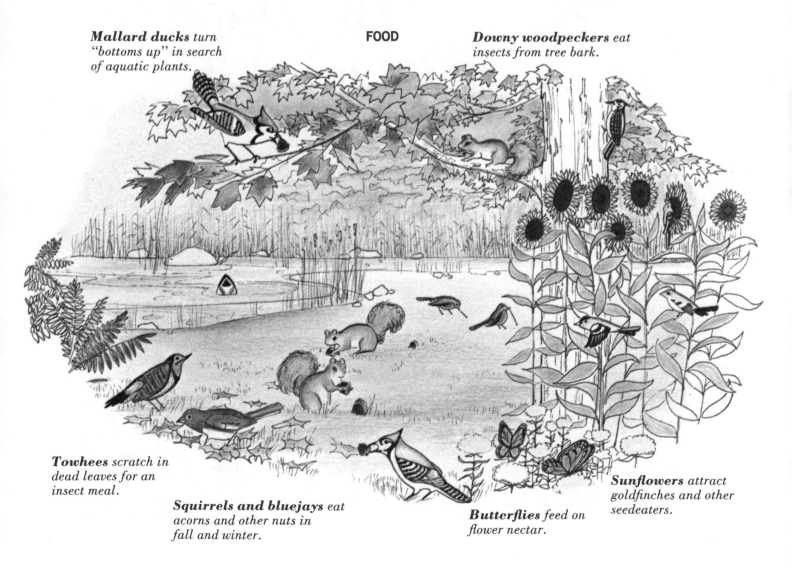

Mallard ducks turn "bottoms up" in search of aquatic plants.

FOOD

Downy woodpeckers eat insects from tree bark.

Towhees scratch in dead leaves for an insect meal.

Squirrels and bluejays eat acorns and other nuts in fall and winter.

Butterflies feed on flower nectar.

Sunflowers attract goldfinches and other seedeaters.

Raccoons, *chiefly nocturnal, feed on frogs, crayfish, and other small creatures.*

Mallards *may visit a pool in spring and fall.*

Turtles *like rocks, and frogs like lily pads, for sunning.*

Killdeer, *a shorebird, may adopt a country pool.*

Frogs and toads *prey on insects and fill the night with a country chorus.*

Redwing blackbirds *build nests among cattails.*

picnic benches upright on the table, to provide a snow screen. Scatter seed underneath the benches. When spring comes, clean the table with a disinfectant before you use it.

If you use feeders, place them in protected places: in a tree, against the wall of your house, under a bush. Make it easy and safe for animals to reach the feeders. And keep the feeders filled with food, especially during the months when snow covers the ground.

Water. A year-round supply of water will attract animals that you wouldn't otherwise see. Animals need water for drinking and bathing. Some animals live in water, at least for part of their lives. Some animals need water to produce mud for nest building.

Water can be provided in a pool, a birdbath, or through a dripping faucet or hose. A pool—for wildlife, not swimming—can be any size and shape. If your ground is hard, you may be able to create a pool by simply

digging out a hole. Or you can dig out a larger hole and line it with plastic sheeting. One family sank an old bathtub into the ground, plugged its outlets, then filled it with water. They added some large rocks that jutted out of the water. Soon, small green frogs were sitting on the rocks. Dragonflies hovered over the pool. Birds came to wash themselves, and every evening a raccoon came to drink.

If you have a pool, plant grass, flowers, and shrubs along its edge. This gives the pool a natural look and provides protective cover for small animals. Water lilies and other aquatic plants can be planted in the pool. Waterlily pads are favorite sunning spots for frogs. And if you put fish, such as goldfish, in your pool, the plants will provide them with oxygen.

Fish are useful as well as interesting to watch. They provide carbon dioxide for aquatic plants. They eat mosquitoes and other pests. Freshwater mussels are useful in pools, too. They eat algae, thereby helping to keep the water clear.

Elevated birdbaths are attractive, and they offer protection from cats. But they will not be used by rabbits, mice, and other small mammals. These need a small pool or a dripping hose or faucet.

The water supply must be dependable. Don't let all the water evaporate during a hot, dry summer. In winter, replace ice in a birdbath with water at least once a day. If you have a pond, keep part of it free of ice. This can be done with a livestock trough warmer, which is available from agricultural supply houses.

Hiding places. Animals need places where they can hide from natural enemies and where they can live during storms and other unpleasant weather. They need places where they can sleep, eat, and loaf.

A pile of branches and other brush is an important part of a backyard habitat. Small animals and game birds use brushpiles to escape from cats, dogs, and other predators. Animals also use the piles as home, especially in places where winters are severe. Place the brushpile in a back corner of your yard, perhaps under some large trees that provide food throughout the winter. The closer an animal's home is to its source of food, the safer it is from predators.

A stone wall or a pile of large rocks provides cover for chipmunks, mice, and lizards. Another excellent hiding place for small animals is an old automobile tire, placed under a bush or among tall grasses. Cut small holes in the lower side of the tire, so rainwater will drain out.

Cats and dogs may be a problem if you are trying to attract wildlife. Fences can be used to keep cats and dogs out of the refuge. You can hide the fences by covering them with

HIDING PLACES

Stone piles for chipmunks and shrubbery for rabbits provide cover from cats and dogs.

Rabbits flee to tall grass when threatened.

Hooded warblers use dense cover to escape from sparrow hawks.

Turtles and frogs find refuge in water.

climbing roses, Virginia creeper, or other vines. And the vines will provide food and resting places for the animals you wish to attract.

Nesting Places. Animals need places where they can reproduce and bear their young. Robins and orioles nest in trees. Catbirds and cardinals nest in dense shrubs. Rabbits nest on the ground, and groundhogs nest in underground burrows.

If your refuge doesn't have enough natural nesting places, you can add nesting boxes. Squirrels, raccoons, and certain birds will use these. Wood ducks, for example, normally nest in old, hollow trees. But they will use a box attached to a tree, especially if the tree is near a pond. The box should be about 1 foot by 1 foot by 2 feet (30 centimeters by 30 centimeters by 60 centimeters) with entrance holes about 4 inches (10 centimeters) in diameter. Put about 5 inches (12 centimeters) of sawdust in the bottom of the box.

Fallen, rotting logs can become living quarters for rabbits, weasels, mink, and other small mammals. Squirrels and chipmunks store winter food in cavities in a log. Beetles feed on the wood. Moles and voles feed on the beetles. A ruffed grouse may use the surface of a log as a stage on which to perform his mating dance.

You can also help nesting animals by providing material for their nests. Save bits of yarn, cord, and thread. In early spring, put these outdoors in a conspicuous place. They will soon be used by eager nest builders.

HOW DO I BEGIN?

To set up a wildlife refuge, you must learn about the animals and plants in your area. Then you should make a plan.

NESTING PLACES

Scarlet tanager's stick nest is flat and usually placed on high branches.

Orioles suspend basket-nests from high branches of mature trees.

Turtles live in water and lay eggs on land near a pool.

Nest boxes for squirrels should be high above the ground.

A pheasant's nest and brood are concealed by tall grass.

Local Animals. To learn which animals live in your area, contact libraries, natural history museums, and state environmental groups. You may discover that there are many interesting animals in your area that you never even knew about—animals that would be very willing to visit you if you were a good host. After you have decided which animals you would like to attract, learn about their needs.

Local Plants. Learn which plants grow best in your area. Learn their water, light, and other needs. Then find out which plants will attract the animals you want, and which will attract the most animals. For example, mountain ash may attract 15 species of birds to your land, but the Eastern red cedar has been known to attract as many as 68 species of birds.

Choose a variety of plants. There should be plants of various heights, shapes, and colors. Choose ones that flower and fruit at different times of the year.

Make a Plan. Draw a diagram of your wildlife refuge. Show how you want it to look. Decide where to place tall trees, short trees, shrubs of various sizes, flowers, and grasses. Decide which plants in your backyard should be transplanted or removed. Decide what you need to buy.

It will take at least several years for the larger plants in your garden to grow to desired sizes. Plan to provide artificial feeding stations and nesting boxes as stopgap measures until there are enough natural food sources and nesting places.

TAKING CARE OF A REFUGE

Maintaining a refuge takes some work. But this is a small price to pay for the pleasures of watching and helping animals.

Perhaps once a year, shrubs and trees need pruning. Pruning helps keep plants attractive, healthy, and productive. Apple trees will produce more and better fruit if they are pruned properly. Flowering shrubs will produce more flowers if they are pruned once a year. Every plant species has its own pruning requirements. Be sure you know when a plant should be pruned and what kind of pruning it needs . . . before you cut.

Pests may be a problem. But don't use pesticides to kill unwanted visitors. Pesticides kill welcome guests as well as pests. For example, pesticides kill honey bees and other insects that pollinate plants. Without pollination, the plants won't produce fruit, which means there will be less food for the wildlife.

To make your garden safe for wildlife, other methods of pest control must be used. Whenever possible, buy plants that are resistant to diseases and pests. Introduce ladybird beetles and praying mantises. These insects feed on pests. If aphids and spider mites attack flowers, wash them off with a strong spray of water from a hose. Provide nesting boxes for tree swallows. These birds feed on many different kinds of insect pests.

Once you begin providing the proper environment for wildlife, you will see many interesting visitors. Keep a wildlife diary. Record the names of visitors. Describe their appearance, their sounds, their behavior. Do robins always appear on the same day in spring? Who is visiting the rose blossoms? When do rabbits and raccoons feed?

What signs of feeding do you see? Look for emptied nut shells, gnawed bark, cut twigs, and places where bark has been peeled from trees.

Torn bark may be a sign that deer are visiting your refuge. Deer will rub their antlers against trees to remove the "velvet." If you find signs of this activity, check the area around the trees in December or January. You may then find the antlers that the deer have shed.

Look for and identify animal tracks. Are opossums and raccoons going to and from the brushpile? Who is drinking from the pond? Animal droppings can also be identified. Owls feed on mice and other small prey. The parts of the food that cannot be digested, such as bones and feathers, are thrown up and spit out in little packets called pellets. If you have attracted an owl to your refuge, look for pellets underneath the tree in which it lives.

As you can see, a backyard refuge can provide you with a great deal of pleasure at the same time that it provides wildlife with a home.

JENNY TESAR
Series Consultant
Wonders of Wildlife

At the Health Education Museum you will see Juno, the transparent talking woman. Juno's body parts light up as she explains the functions of all your body systems.

ON DISPLAY: THE HUMAN BODY

See the transparent woman and listen to her talk . . . walk into the center of a giant tooth . . . examine a human skull . . . watch doctors and nurses in an operating room.

You can do all these things—and much more—at the Cleveland Health Education Museum in Ohio. The Museum is devoted entirely to the human body. There are more than 150 different things to see and do. It's a wonderful place to learn a lot—and have lots of fun at the same time.·

One section in the museum is called the Children's Health Fair. There, Howie the Hound and other animals will tell you about nutrition and the five senses. You can introduce yourself to Ophelia the Octopus and shake all of her eight "hands." Or sit under the ear of Pinky the Elephant. Or check your height against the long neck of Ginny the Giraffe.

In the Gebhard Theater you will find Juno, the transparent talking woman. Juno explains the functions of all your body systems, and her body parts light up as she tells you about them. Juno rotates on an illuminated platform, which allows you to see the body parts from all sides. If you want an even closer look, the room also contains transparent models of the nine body systems.

In the Theater of Vision, you walk into the center of a human eye and find out how the eye is put together and how it works. You learn about common eye problems, and you can even test your own eyesight. In the Theater of Hearing, you learn how your ears work and how to preserve your hearing. (One hint: loud music and other loud sounds can damage your ears.) You can also test your hearing and see what your voice looks like in sound waves.

And how about your teeth? Are you taking proper care of them? Find out from the Giant Tooth. You can walk right into the center of this huge, 18-foot (5.5-meter) molar. Once inside, you hear a program that explains tooth structure and why dental health is so important.

Everyone is interested in why we are what we are. As you wander around the Giant Chromosome Puff, you will hear the fascinating story of heredity. Then walk into the puff and learn about DNA, the chemical that carries all your heredity information.

The environment can affect your body and your health in many ways. The environment consists of everything around you, including other living things. Some of the organisms that have the biggest effects on people are so tiny that they can only be seen through powerful microscopes. These are microbes. In the museum's Microbe Alley, some of these microbes have been turned into giant models. There are colorful plastic sculptures of bacteria, fungi, and molds. And if you want to compare these models with the real thing, just look through the microscopes set up in Microbe Alley, and you'll see different kinds of micro-organisms.

After this, you'll want to learn how to prevent illness and fight germs at the Defense of Life exhibit. A maze of tubes and lights, forming a giant model of blood vessels, represents a patch of human tissue magnified 64,000 times. You'll learn how blood cells and chemicals called enzymes protect you against infection and disease.

And there's still more. Press a button and see what happens inside your body when a splinter enters your skin . . . or take a seat in a revolving theater and view the Electronic Brain. It shows how the brain receives, records, and reacts to messages sent to it by your five senses. Or visit the Surgical Theater, which shows a team of doctors and nurses performing a hip operation. They're models, of course, but so realistic that you'll think you are actually in a hospital operating room.

Learning how your body works and what to do to keep it running smoothly is important. Remember, you've got to live with your body for the rest of your life. Treat it well, and your life will be longer and happier.

Soaring high into the air is the golden Sunsphere, symbol of the 1982 World's Fair in Knoxville.

THE 1982 WORLD'S FAIR

In 1982, millions of people traveled to Knoxville, Tennessee. From May through October, Knoxville played host to the Knoxville International Energy Exposition—better known as the 1982 World's Fair. It was the first world's fair to focus on energy as a theme.

Soaring 266 feet (81 meters) above the fairground was the Sunsphere, the symbol of the fair. This structure was a monument to the sun—the greatest energy source of all. The Sunsphere looked like a giant gold golf ball resting on a blue steel tee. The globe at the top was made of glass containing real gold dust. Inside this golden sphere were a restaurant and observation decks, from which you could view the city of Knoxville and the nearby Great Smoky Mountains.

THE EXHIBITS

Thirteen separate countries and the ten-member European Community presented exhibits reflecting the fair's theme, ''Energy Turns the World.'' These exhibitors also devoted space to history, culture, arts, crafts, and folklore.

• **Australia** displayed working windmills and solar energy devices. The exhibit also had moving sidewalks and Australian eucalyptus and fern trees.

• **Japan** brought talking robots that discussed the world's energy problems. And there were models of energy-efficient cities of the future.

• The **United States** had a large pavilion that was solar-powered. There were computers that talked back to visitors, and robots. A film called *Energy! Energy!* was shown on a screen seven stories tall.

• **Hungary** displayed the world's largest Rubik's Cube. This famous puzzle was invented by the Hungarian architect Ernö Rubik. The cube in the Hungarian exhibit was unlike any you may have played with. It was huge—each side was 6 feet (2 meters) across. And the cube was motorized. It twisted and turned and solved itself mechanically several times a minute.

• **China** took part in a world's fair for the first time since 1904. There were life-size statues of warriors and horses from the tomb of an ancient emperor. And there were ancient bricks from the Great Wall. It was the first time that part of the wall had been allowed out of China. Art objects included tapestries, elaborate carvings in jade and ivory, and hand-painted porcelain. The Chinese also gave rides on a solar-powered dragon boat. The boat had two large canopies made of solar cells, which collected the sun's energy and changed it into electricity to run the boat.

• **Other national exhibits** displayed many variations on the energy theme. Britain focused on new energy sources for the "post-oil" age. Canada used videodiscs, comput-

At the U.S. pavilion, you could "shake hands" with a robot.

23

ers, and films to describe its projects in energy use and conservation. The Republic of Korea demonstrated "ondol," a hot-floor heating system that has been used since prehistoric times. West Germany's exhibit included models of an 18th-century waterwheel and a 20th-century nuclear reactor.

There were also exhibits from corporations, states, the city of Knoxville, and several organizations.

• The **Union Carbide Corporation** exhibit included a collection of battery-powered games and toys, which visitors were invited to operate. Some of the games taught arithmetic and spelling. The toys included dogs that barked and bears that played musical instruments. There was even a roller coaster that gave rides to Mickey Mouse and his friends.

• The **Tennessee Valley Authority (TVA),** located in the Knoxville area, is the largest public utility in the United States. At the TVA exhibit, a computer game let visitors pretend they were operating a TVA power system. They had to decide what kinds of power to use to meet consumer demands. If they made a mistake, the computer told them how much money it cost the consumers.

TECHNOLOGY FOR TOMORROW AND TODAY

World's fairs are places to see the world of tomorrow—today. At the Paris World's Fair in 1867, aluminum was introduced. And visitors tasted the world's first ice cream sodas. At the Philadelphia World's Fair in 1876, the telephone and the typewriter made their debuts. Television was unveiled at the 1939 New York World's Fair.

The Knoxville fair continued this tradition. There were futuristic cars, models of futuristic cities, and solar-powered telephones. A new kind of milk was introduced. The milk is pasteurized at very high temperatures. This makes it possible to store the milk without refrigeration for more than three months.

At the U.S. exhibit, a new computer technology was introduced. It involved a computer hooked up to a video screen. If you wanted to know more about a term that was shown on the screen, you simply touched the screen where the term appeared. The computer then retrieved the information and displayed it on the screen.

Some exhibits gave visitors energy-saving ideas that they could use today in their own homes. A remodeled Victorian house con-

tained devices that could reduce energy consumption. There were explanations on how to install and use the devices. A transparent house in the U.S. pavilion allowed people to actually see energy-saving features and how they are added to existing houses.

Another energy-saving house, called the House of the Future, was a geodesic dome. This type of building looks somewhat like an igloo. Less energy is needed to heat a geodesic dome than a conventional house because a dome exposes less exterior surface to the weather. Most of the power used by the House of the Future was provided by a propeller windmill. Solar panels on the dome's roof provided some electricity and heated water.

FAIR AND FESTIVAL

Almost everywhere visitors went at the fair, they were entertained. Magicians, mimes, and jugglers dressed in brightly colored costumes strolled through the fair site. A daily parade featured the World's Fair Marching Band and high school bands from all over the United States. At night, there were fireworks and a laser sky show that could be seen for miles.

The Folklife Festival presented the life and culture of the southern Appalachian region. Skilled artisans demonstrated crafts that included quilting, weaving, chair caning, and blacksmithing. Visitors could watch a cook cleaning dandelion greens and boiling up a batch of hog intestines for chitlins. And with a little luck, the hungry audiences were even able to sample some freshly baked corn bread.

Old-fashioned entertainment was another feature of the popular Folklife Festival. Musicians played bluegrass and country-and-western music. There were clog dancers, square dancers, fiddling contests, and gospel singers.

The fair also included an amusement area. Visitors could play the latest video games. They could ride on a double-deck carousel and a high-speed roller coaster. And they could climb aboard the giant Pirate Ship, which was styled after a 17th-century pirate galleon.

The people who visited the 1982 World's Fair will long remember it. And the stories told by the many exhibits will affect all of us. For, as the fair proclaimed, "Energy Turns the World."

A Canadian exhibit showed energy-saving advances in automobile design.

THE MESSY DESK

What does your desk look like? Is it neat and clean with lots of room on which to write and work? Or is it as messy as the desk shown here?

You will find 34 items on this desk. But they are all hidden in the search-a-word puzzle. Cover the puzzle with a sheet of tracing paper. Read forward, backward, up, down, and diagonally. Then shade in the letters of each item as you find it. One item has been shaded in for you.

Some letters will be left over after you have found all the items. With a colored pencil, circle all the unused letters. If you read them from left to right, you will find a hidden message. The message tells you what the famous U.S. Supreme Court Justice Felix Frankfurter once said about desks—although your parents may not agree!

apple
bicycle lock
blotter
brush
calculator
calendar
candy cane
clock
coins

crayons
daffodils
dictionary
eraser
frisbee
glue
key
lamp
letter

magic markers
paper clips
pencil
photograph
rubber bands
rubiks cube
ruler
scissors
seashell

shoelace
stapler
tape
teddy bear
telephone
tennis ball
turtle

M	C	A	N	D	Y	C	A	N	E	A	C	L	T	E	S
R	A	H	P	A	R	G	O	T	O	H	P	A	E	P	H
E	L	G	P	A	P	E	R	C	L	I	P	S	D	A	O
L	C	E	I	K	C	O	L	C	A	P	D	D	D	T	E
U	U	L	I	C	N	E	P	P	L	N	B	I	Y	K	L
R	L	N	D	E	M	S	S	E	A	K	R	C	B	C	A
R	A	D	N	E	L	A	C	B	R	T	U	T	E	O	C
U	T	U	R	T	L	E	R	I	E	P	S	I	A	L	E
B	O	R	E	L	R	E	A	K	S	S	H	O	R	E	E
I	R	N	A	A	B	T	Y	G	E	S	S	N	F	L	B
K	A	M	S	B	N	E	O	L	A	R	O	A	R	C	L
S	P	E	U	M	P	T	N	U	S	Y	S	R	I	Y	O
C	R	R	C	O	I	N	S	E	H	K	M	Y	S	C	T
U	L	L	A	B	S	I	N	N	E	T	E	I	B	I	T
B	N	D	A	F	F	O	D	I	L	S	D	Y	E	B	E
E	N	O	H	P	E	L	E	T	L	E	T	T	E	R	R

MESSAGE: A clean desk represents an empty mind.

27

This kudzu vine has engulfed an oak tree and looks like a green monster that is going to invade Atlanta, Georgia.

THE KUDZU INVASION

Picture this scene: A huge green vine creeps silently over the land. It covers houses, cars, trees, and everything else in its path. People battle the vine, trying to stop its advance. They hack at it, dig at its roots, and spray it with chemicals. But it's a tough fight.

A horror movie? No. It's happening now, in the southern part of the United States.

The vine is the kudzu, a native of Asia. It was introduced into the United States in 1876, as the nation celebrated its 100th birthday. A big centennial fair, with exhibits from many nations, was held in Philadelphia. The Japanese planted a kudzu vine to decorate their exhibit. Americans admired the vine, with its large, soft, grassy green leaves and clusters of reddish-purple flowers. They asked the Japanese for kudzu seeds and seedlings, which they planted in their gardens. By the early 1900's, the plant was quite common in the South.

At first, there were many friends of the kudzu. The vine got its most important support beginning in the 1930's. At that time, soil erosion was a serious problem in many places. Productive farms with rich soil had turned into eroded hills and gullies of red clay. To make the land productive again, huge amounts of nitrogen needed to be added to the soil. Soil conservationists believed that the kudzu could do this. The kudzu is a member of the pea family of plants. These plants put nitrogen into the soil as they grow.

By the 1950's, over 70,000,000 kudzu seedlings had been planted. As promised, the plants stopped erosion and enriched the soil. They provided food for farm animals. They even beautified the land by covering up litter, abandoned cars, and other unsightly objects.

But one big difference between Japan and the American South is climate. In Japan, the winters are cold. Freezing temperatures kill the kudzu vines, even though the plant's underground roots remain alive. In the American South, winters are generally much warmer than those in Japan. Rarely are there killing frosts. For the kudzu, it's like living in a big greenhouse. In Japan, the kudzu also has natural enemies that limit its growth. There are no such enemies in the American South.

In the South, the vines began to grow out of control and cover everything in their path. They killed trees and other plants. By the 1960's, Americans had stopped planting kudzu. Instead, they were trying to get rid of the plants. This, however, has not been an easy thing to do. The kudzu grows about a foot a day. Each plant has a monstrous root. It's rather like a carrot, but much, much bigger. A kudzu root can weigh 400 pounds (180 kilograms). As many as 50 vines may grow from one root, and each vine may be 100 feet (30 meters) long.

People are sending cows into kudzu fields to eat the vines. They are also trying to dig up the huge roots. And they are spraying chemical weed-killers on the kudzu. But getting rid of the plant is proving to be a slow and costly job. For the people of the American South, the kudzu vine has become a botanical nightmare.

28

A VERY FAT TREE

On the dry plains of tropical Africa lives a tree called the baobab. Its most distinctive feature is its size. It isn't exceptionally tall. But it is exceptionally fat. Few other trees are as fat as a baobab.

Baobab trunks look like swollen barrels. The average diameter ranges from 30 to 60 feet (9 to 18 meters). But many baobabs are even larger. One baobab trunk is said to have a diameter of 100 feet (30 meters). These sizes are bigger than the rooms in most people's houses. A baobab trunk is big enough to live in, which is exactly what some Africans have done. They have hollowed out the trunk and use the baobab as their home. Others use hollowed trunks as places to store grain or water—or to stay dry during a thunderstorm. The hollowed-out trunk of a large baobab can shelter as many as 30 people.

There are many more uses for the baobab. Fiber from the bark is used to make fishnets, rope, fabric, packing paper, and even musical instruments. The fiber is very strong. In Bengal, there is a saying, "As secure as an elephant bound with a baobab rope."

Baobab wood, however, is soft and light in weight. One author wrote that a high-speed bullet from a rifle will pass right through the trunk, in spite of its great thickness. The wood is used to make dugout canoes and floats for fishing nets.

Young baobab leaves are eaten as a vegetable. The fruit is also eaten. A baobab fruit is shaped like a fat sausage that is thicker in the middle than at the ends. It is 6 to 12 inches (15 to 30 centimeters) long. The pulp of the fruit, which has a pleasant but somewhat dry taste, is called monkey bread. It is eaten raw, or it is dried and mixed with water to make a lemonade-like drink. The seeds are ground and used as a fertilizer. Sometimes the ground seeds may be used as a food, particularly when other foods are scarce.

Another interesting fact about the baobab is that, unlike the trunks of other trees, its trunk doesn't get thicker every year. Sometimes it gets smaller. The weather seems to determine whether the tree expands or shrinks. In years when there is a lot of rain, the baobab gets thicker. During droughts, it gets thinner.

A relative of the baobab that grows in Australia is sometimes called the bottle tree. It is slightly smaller than the African baobab, but it has an equally remarkable shape. And like the baobab, it has a long life span. One bottle tree in northern Australia is believed to be 2,000 years old. Its hollow trunk was once used as a jail.

Today, the baobab and the bottle tree can be found far from their native lands. People in other tropical and semitropical areas are cultivating these trees because they are so unusual.

The huge trunk of a baobab tree is big enough to live in.

VIDEO FEVER

He has a yellow body, a huge mouth, and no eyes or nose. But despite his looks, this little fellow is one of the most popular guys around. His name is Pac-Man. And millions of people spend time playing with him.

Pac-Man lives in a maze. By moving a joystick, you can make Pac-Man run. Up and down the corridors he races, gobbling up little white dots. Watch out! Four colorful ghosts are chasing him. If one of the ghosts catches Pac-Man, it will eat him. But if you can get Pac-Man to one of the large energy dots, the ghosts will turn blue for a short time—and Pac-Man can eat them.

Your score climbs higher and higher. But suddenly your little friend gets cornered by two of the ghosts . . . end of game! Your score—3,280 points—sounds pretty good. But then you notice a sign at the top of the machine: HIGH SCORE—56,540. So you grab the joystick and try again.

VIDEO VARIETY

Pac-Man is just one of hundreds of video games that are now the rage all over the world. These are some of the most popular variations:

• Space games: Take command of a spaceship . . . fight aliens from outer space . . . dodge meteors . . . break up asteroids.

• War games: Drive a tank . . . pilot a World War I biplane . . . protect cities from a missile attack.

• Fantasy games: Break down the walls of your opponent's castle . . . battle spiders, snakes, and other evil creatures . . . keep away from monsters that want to eat you . . . hunt for hidden treasure.

• Sports games: Play football or baseball . . . drive a sports car . . . shoot pool . . . try your hand at tennis.

Some of the games are easy to play. Others are highly complex. Many can be played at several levels of difficulty—you can begin at an easy level and move to more difficult levels as you become more skilled.

Some games are designed for one player. Others can be played by two or more people, in competition against one another. Many games offer several options—playing by yourself, against another person, or against a computer.

Video games can be played at home or in arcades. Home games are played on a video-game machine or a computer. These machines attach to a TV set, which displays the game on the screen. The game itself is on a cartridge, tape cassette, or disk, which is put into the machine.

Arcade games are coin-operated. A quarter buys you at least a few minutes of time on a game. Depending on your skill and luck, you may be able to play a lot longer.

CONTROVERSIAL BUT FUN

Video games are a favorite of young people. (In fact, teenagers generally get much higher scores than adults.) Because children are spending so much time with video games, the games have become almost as controversial as they are popular. Some people think they are a bad influence on children. Others think video games are valuable for children.

The Critics Say . . . Video games are time-wasters. Children tend to spend too much time playing them, which takes away from other recreational activities and study time.

Many video games are really war games, since the object is to destroy a menacing obstacle before it destroys you. Because of their violent nature, the games will cause aggressive behavior among the youngsters who play them.

Video games are addictive. Players rarely play just once. They keep at it, trying to get higher and higher scores. And as soon as players have mastered one game, they move on to another one.

The Supporters Say . . . Video games build concentration.They demand total attention. If your mind wanders, you will soon be hit by a blast from an enemy ship or caught by a gobbling ghost.

The games improve reflexes and develop eye-hand co-ordination. Many provide mental challenges. To do well, players must work out strategies. They must discover patterns and solve problems.

Video games give children who are not athletic a chance to succeed at something their friends admire. Being accepted for a particular skill helps build confidence.

The games are a good way to be introduced to computers. This is valuable because computers are quickly becoming an important part of everyday life. One sociologist says, "The kids are learning that computers are something you approach without intimidation, hands first, and take control of."

Despite all the controversy, if you ask young people what they think about video games, you'll get the most obvious answer: "I love them, they're fun."

A BIG BUSINESS

People are spending billions of dollars a year on video games. Still more money is being spent on home video machines, computers, and a variety of "spin-offs"—products that are associated with the games.

Video games are played at home on a video-game machine or a computer, which can be attached to a TV set. The game itself is on a cartridge, tape cassette, or disk.

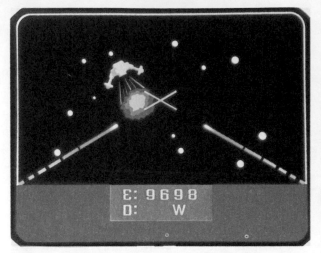

There are many video games, such as StarMaster . . .

. . . Fishing Derby . . .

. . . Frog Bog . . .

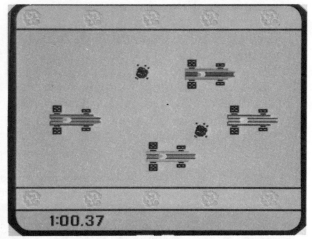

. . . Grand Prix . . .

. . . and Donkey Kong.

These include T-shirts, greeting cards, board games, comics, mugs, watches, and dolls. There is a chewing gum named for the popular space game Asteroids. A hit record album of 1982 was *Pac-Man Fever*.

People are also buying a variety of books that explain how to play video games. The books describe specific games and offer hints on how to get high scores.

In 1982, the Hollywood movie studios got into the act. They began making video games based on movies. Among the first such games were those based on *TRON,* a movie about a deadly battle inside a computer.

Are video games a fad that will soon disappear, or are they here to stay? No one really knows. But many companies and game designers are betting that they will be around for a long time. And at the rate that people are buying the games—and playing them in the arcades—it looks as if the companies are on the right track.

VIDEO-GAME ARCADES

Colorful lights flash. Strange beeping sounds are heard. Odd names are seen—Gorf, Donkey Kong, Asteroids, Centipede, Defender, Frogger, Battle Zone. The video-game arcades have invaded. And the way Pac-Man gobbles up dots, the coin-operated machines in the arcades gobble up quarters.

Video-game arcades have exploded in popularity. And in towns and cities everywhere, many people are complaining. They include people who don't object to home video games but do object to video-game arcades. Why are the video game arcades causing even more controversy than the video games themselves?

Parents complain that students are skipping school to play at the arcades. They also say that their children are spending too much money—usually allowances and lunch money—in the arcades. They feel that the money could be better spent on other activities. Youngsters admit that it takes $20 or more to become good at many arcade games. But they say they would rather spend their money on the games than on the movies.

People also complain that arcades are often undesirable environments—that they are "hangouts" for drinking, drug abuse, and gambling. They say the arcades cause disruptive behavior and an increase in crime. Supporters say that the trouble is not with the arcades but with a few problem youngsters. These teenagers cause the same trouble at some arcades that they would cause in other places in the community.

The controversy goes on. The coin-operated machines have spread to restaurants, bowling alleys, gas stations, and other commercial establishments. Many communities want their local governments to do something—to pass laws prohibiting the machines altogether, or to regulate where, when, and by whom they can be played. Some communities have already passed such laws. Supporters of the machines say the laws violate the constitutional rights of players and store owners.

What do you think? Are arcades and other places that have coin-operated video games good or bad for a community and its children?

Some sea anemones live in colonies.

Clownfish are safe among an anemone's poisonous tentacles.

FLOWER ANIMALS OF THE SEA

In the soft sand and mud of quiet bays, along wharf pilings, and in the rocky tidal pools at the edge of the sea dwells a group of creatures that look like lovely flowers. Many of them resemble exotic dahlias or chrysanthemums. But these creatures were named after another flower—the anemone. And while sea anemones may look like gentle flowers, they are animals whose petal-like tentacles are armed with poisonous cells.

Sea anemones belong to a group of water animals called coelenterates. This group also includes corals, jellyfish, and hydroids. The name coelenterate, meaning ''hollow gut,'' was given to these animals because each of them is basically a hollow sac with a single opening, the mouth, surrounded by tentacles.

There are more than 800 different species of sea anemone, and they live in every ocean in the world. They can be found at great depths, but they prefer shallow waters near shore. Many live on coral reefs. Most anemones live singly, but some form colonies.

Anemones living with red sponges.

Sea anemones come in a dazzling array of colors, shapes, and sizes. Some are scarcely larger than your fingernail. Others are more than 3 feet (1 meter) across. Their striking hues can range from a vivid red, or yellow and red striped, to a deep green.

The body of the anemone is shaped like a cylinder—some broad and short, others tall and slender. At the base of the cylinder is a slimy, muscular disk that the anemone uses to attach itself to rocks, shells, or wharf pilings. Anemones can also glide along on their disks like snails. At the upper end of the cylinder is the mouth opening. This opening is surrounded by one or more circles of hollow tentacles. Each of the tentacles is armed with thousands of poisonous stinging cells.

An anemone closed up, with only its mouth showing.

An anemone wide open, showing its digestive cavity.

If a crab or fish touches a tentacle, it is paralyzed by the cells. Then the victim is passed by the tentacles through the mouth into a large cavity where it is digested.

Sea anemones have unusual relationships with certain other marine animals. They have been known to cling to jellyfish, attach themselves to sponges, and live with crabs. But the anemone's most remarkable relationship is with the clownfish. This colorful little fish fearlessly darts among the anemone's poisonous tentacles and sleeps nestled in them at night. How does the clownfish avoid becoming dinner? It seems that it disguises itself by becoming coated with mucus from the anemone. The anemone doesn't perceive the clownfish as a tasty morsel, but as part of itself. And so without even knowing it, the anemone becomes the protector of the clownfish—which probably couldn't survive for long on its own because it is a poor swimmer.

The next time you visit the seashore, look closely into the quiet rocky pools and you just may see the slowly waving tentacles of a colorful sea anemone. But be careful. It's not a gentle flower.

PETER D. CAPEN
Executive Director
The Whale Museum and Orca Society

A GRIM FAIRY TALE

One evening in January, the Seven Dwarfs hurried through their after-dinner chores. They had a special guest. Snow White had come to visit them for a few days, and she had brought a brand-new book of scary stories.

Now, the Dwarfs loved Snow White's stories even more than they loved her pies. And as soon as the last dish had been put away, they quickly took their places around her chair by the fireplace.

Everyone wanted to be close to the Princess, who was a wonderful storyteller. She read every word with expression. The Dwarfs agreed that if a story was told by Snow White, it always seemed to be true.

The Princess opened the beautiful leather-bound book. "Once upon a time there lived a wicked wizard named Waldo," she began. "His favorite pastime was turning people into toads."

"Toads?" whispered Bashful.

"Yes, toads," answered Snow White. "He would wave his wand and cry, 'Snippety-snee! A toad you'll be!' And some poor person would hop off to hide in a damp corner of the wizard's castle."

As Snow White was telling her tale, it got darker and darker. The only light in the cottage came from the fireplace. The flickering flames made shadows leap and play on the walls. Every time the wizard changed someone into a toad and Snow White repeated the magic rhyme, the Dwarfs would look fearfully about, as if they expected a wizard to jump out of one of their cupboards. Finally, Doc got up and locked the door.

"Humbug," grumped Grumpy. "I don't know what you ninnies are so scared about. It's just a story." But even Grumpy only half believed his brave words.

Finally the scary tale came to an end, but not before the wizard had turned practically everyone into a toad. Snow White closed her book.

"Did you enjoy the story?" she asked the Dwarfs. They were standing up, but still huddled together, looking uneasily around the darkened cottage.

"Heh-heh," Doc laughed nervously. "Sure, Princess. It was a state glory, er . . . great story."

Then Sleepy, who wasn't at all sleepy, piped up. "It *was* only a story, wasn't it?"

"Well," began Snow White.

"Of course it was only a story," scoffed Grumpy, brave once more, now that the tale was over. "There's no such thing as a wizard. Right, Princess?"

Snow White replied with a twinkle in her eye. "Maybe there isn't . . . and maybe there is." Then she yawned. "I think it's time we went to bed."

"Oh . . . right," answered Happy. "You can have our bedroom, as usual, ma'am. We'll be plenty comfortable down here."

"Sure," added Doc. "We'll fee bine, er . . . be fine. Goodnight, Princess."

Soon the Dwarfs heard the door to the bedroom softly close. Still they stood there, close together, looking at one another.

"Well, now," said Doc with false heartiness. "Let's ded bown, er . . . bed down, men."

Sleepy looked nervously around. "But I'm not sleepy," he protested.

37

"Humbug," said Grumpy. "You're always sleepy. Just lie down and quit jumpin' at shadows."

So the Seven Dwarfs settled down in their makeshift beds—Happy in a cupboard, Doc in the sink, Grumpy in the kettle, Bashful in a drawer, and Sneezy on the woodpile. Sleepy stretched out next to Dopey on a bench, even though he was as wide awake as he'd ever been. All seven little men stirred restlessly, but soon the room was filled with the sounds of six dwarfs softly snoring.

Six? Yes, six. Because Sleepy was still having trouble falling asleep. He kept thinking he heard toads' feet plopping damply across the floor, but it was only the faucet dripping on Doc's chest. Then, in his mind's eye, he pictured Waldo the wizard creeping up to the cottage.

Sleepy gave a quick glance at the window, and, sure enough, there was a shadow of something looking in.

Very quietly, Sleepy got up, careful not to wake Dopey. He stole over to the door and slipped outside, closing the door behind him with a small *snick!*

Moonlight bathed the clearing. A wind had sprung up, and branches whipped about, casting strange shadows. Sleepy stood just outside the door, trying to work up the nerve to investigate the window.

Finally he summoned the courage to creep to the corner and peer around it. Then he breathed a sigh of relief. Now that he was outside, he could see that it was only a pine branch that made the wizard-shaped shadow.

Congratulating himself on his courage, Sleepy reminded himself that, after all, the story had been only a story. He strutted back to the door. He took hold of the knob and turned it, but the door wouldn't budge!

Inside the cottage, however, Dopey was becoming gradually aware that Sleepy wasn't in his place on the bench. Rubbing his eyes, the little dwarf sat up and looked around for his friend. He counted one, two, three, four, five other dwarfs asleep in the room, but no Sleepy.

Dopey got up and tiptoed over and woke Happy. He gestured wildly at the bench. He alternated between pantomiming Sleepy's name with hands clasped underneath his cheek and shrugging to mean that he didn't know where Sleepy was.

"It's Sleepy," Happy translated finally. "You can't find Sleepy!"

Dopey nodded vigorously.

"We'd better wake the others," said Happy, getting up briskly.

"What's wrong?" mumbled Doc.

"What in tarnation?" growled Grumpy.

"Sleepy's missin'," said Happy.

"The wizard!" gasped Bashful. "He's turned him into a toad!"

"Humbug!" scoffed Grumpy. "There's no such thing as a wizard!"

"Then where's Sleepy?" challenged Sneezy.

"He's probably just outside," answered Grumpy. "He was havin' trouble gettin' to sleep. Come on!" And he led the dwarfs outside.

They found the clearing empty. Suddenly there was a *plop! plop!* sound. A great big toad was hopping slowly across the clearing on his way to the stream. He had suspiciously sleepy-looking eyes.

"Sleepy!" cried Grumpy, finally convinced. He scooped the toad up in his arms. "He's turned you into a toad!"

"No!" chorused Doc, Bashful, Sneezy and Happy. Dopey clapped his hands to his face in horror.

"Who's turned who into a toad?" came the muffled query from the hollow tree. Sleepy poked his head out, eyes blinking in the strong moonlight. "Can't a fellow get some sleep around here?"

"Why, you old—" began Grumpy.

"Now, now," soothed Doc. "I'm sure there's a ferpectly, er . . . perfectly good explanation here."

"Let's hear it," scowled Grumpy. He crossed his arms and glared at Sleepy.

Everyone felt foolish when Sleepy explained how he had locked himself out and taken shelter in the hollow tree. "That Snow White," Sleepy finished admiringly. "She's just too good a storyteller for me!"

"Make that all of us," said Happy. "She had us all believin' in that wicked wizard fellow."

"You're right," admitted Grumpy. "Next time she visits, I think we'd better tell her to leave the scary stories at home and bring the nursery rhymes!"

Umbrellas and parasols have been used all over the world for centuries. This picture of a parasol vendor, from *Merchants of the Mysterious East* by John Lim, shows some parasols that can really turn heads.

THE UNSUNG UMBRELLA

"Where is my toadstool?" loud he lamented.
And that's how umbrellas were first invented!
The Elf and the Dormouse, Oliver Herford

The umbrella you hold over your head on a rainy day—with its bright fabric stretched taut over shiny metal ribs—certainly seems a modern object. But in fact, umbrellas and parasols have been used for more than 3,000 years. Our word "umbrella" comes from the Latin word *umbra*, which means "shade." "Parasol" comes from *parere* and *sol*— "shield" and "sun." Today people use an umbrella as a shield against rain, and a parasol as a sunshade.

No one knows when or where the first umbrellas and parasols were made, but it is known that they were used in ancient Egypt and Assyria. There they were a privilege awarded to royalty. Umbrellas were held over pharoahs and kings for the practical purpose of shielding the ruler from the sun. But the umbrellas also had religious and mythological meaning. They represented the dome of heaven and indicated the ruler's closeness to the gods. As shown in sculptures, the ancient Egyptian umbrellas were heavy, cumbersome things—the royal umbrella bearer had to use both hands to hold up the thick shaft.

Umbrellas and parasols were also known in ancient Greece, and there, too, they had religious significance. Parasols were carried in processions and used in festivals honoring the goddess Persephone and the god Dionysus. But they were also used as everyday sunshades by Greek women.

Before 200 B.C., the use of the parasol spread from Greece to Rome. Roman women regarded the parasol strictly as a useful—and fashionable—accessory, without religious meaning. A Roman parasol might have an ivory, gem-studded handle and a bright purple cover decorated with gold. Some women dyed their parasols various colors to show which teams they favored in the chariot races.

Umbrellas and parasols have been used in China and other Far Eastern countries for at least as long as in the West. Early Chinese umbrellas and parasols were far ahead of the Western ones in design—they had collapsible ribs so that they could be opened and shut, and some had telescoping handles. The handles were often made of bamboo, with colored silk and paper for the covers.

By the time of the Ming dynasty (A.D. 1368–1644) in China, elaborate rules of etiquette determined what kind of umbrella a person could bear. The emperor was normally accompanied by twelve umbrella bearers. Provincial governors and high-ranking military officers could bear two red silk umbrellas. The highest ranking nobles had umbrellas of black gauze, with red silk linings and three flounces. Gentlemen had umbrellas of red or blue cloth, depending on their rank, while ordinary people were restricted to umbrellas of oiled paper.

Umbrellas were used in funeral and wedding rites in India, and an Indian legend tells that the god Brahma held a white umbrella over Buddha's head when he was born. In Burma, white umbrellas were reserved for the king, one of whose many titles was "Lord of the Parasols." His state umbrellas were about 15 feet (4.5 meters) tall. An umbrella bearer also accompanied the Mikado, the ruler of Japan.

In Africa, kings proclaimed their dignity with huge, brilliantly colored state umbrellas. Many were decorated with tassels, fringes, and appliquéd designs. European ex-

A scene from a Greek vase, made about 450 B.C., shows a parasol at the feast of the Greek god Dionysus.

The Japanese have used bamboo parasols with collapsible ribs since early times. This print is from the 1700's.

In some cultures, umbrellas have long been a symbol of royalty. Shown here are a Biblical king and queen in a 13th-century mosaic (*left*), and Queen Mary of England in Africa in 1924.

In the 1600's, when this print was made, fashionable Frenchwomen carried parasols on their outdoor strolls.

plorers of the 1700's reported that one African king's umbrella was decorated with human jawbones and topped by a skull. An African umbrella brought to Britain in the 1800's had a circumference of about 22 feet (6.5 meters).

In Europe, most people regarded umbrellas and parasols as practical items. During the Middle Ages and the Renaissance, they were used mainly as sunshades in southern areas—Italy, Spain, and Portugal—by both men and women. The pope had an umbrella for ceremonial use, however, and in the 1100's the doge of Venice was awarded the privilege of bearing a state umbrella.

Umbrellas and parasols didn't become popular in northern Europe until the 1600's, when the French nobility began to carry parasols. In the 1630's the French king Louis XIII had a collection of eleven taffeta parasols and three umbrellas of oiled cloth, trimmed with gold and silver lace. By 1700, umbrellas and parasols were being produced in large numbers for everyone's use. One Parisian manufacturer even offered a pocket parasol—it had folding ribs and a shaft that could be taken apart in three sections. And as umbrellas became more popular, they lost their association with the upper classes. In the 1760's a French nobleman noted that people "who do not wish to be taken as belonging to the vulgar herd, prefer to risk a wetting . . . for an umbrella is a sure sign that one possesses no carriage."

Despite their popularity in France, umbrellas and parasols were still considered oddities in Britain. A few umbrellas were kept in coffee houses, to shelter patrons on their way from the door to their carriages on rainy days. Some fashionable women carried parasols. But when a man named Jonas Hanway began to carry his umbrella in the streets of London in the late 1700's, he caused a sensation. He was ridiculed for carrying a contraption that was considered feminine. And he was criticized for defying the "heavenly purpose" of rain—which was to make people wet.

Umbrellas caused no less a stir when they were introduced in Britain's North American colonies. A Connecticut woman who carried an umbrella was mocked by her neighbors, who copied her by carrying sieves balanced

In *The Umbrellas,* a painting by Pierre Auguste Renoir, umbrellas crowd a Paris street of the 1800's.

on broomsticks. A Philadelphia man caused such a disturbance with his umbrella that the town watch was called out.

But by 1800, umbrellas were becoming common in Britain and in America. British Army officers became so attached to their umbrellas that in the Napoleonic Wars they sometimes carried them into battle—until the Duke of Wellington ordered a stop to the practice. By the middle of the 1800's, an umbrella was considered a necessary accessory for any gentleman. The author Robert Louis Stevenson wrote, "It is the habitual carriage of the umbrella that is the stamp of Respectability. The umbrella has become the acknowledged index of social position."

Most umbrellas of the early 1800's were unwieldy, with spans of 4 feet (1.2 meters) or more. Their oiled or waxed cloth covers often leaked. With a wooden handle and whalebone ribs, an umbrella might weigh as much as 10 pounds (4.5 kilograms). These umbrellas were so hard to handle that walking down a crowded city street on a windy, rainy day could be hazardous.

In the 1800's, a well-dressed American woman could choose from a wide variety of parasols in the latest styles.

By the mid-1800's, smaller, lighter models were being made, with frames of steel. Novelty designs were also introduced. Handles were hollowed out to conceal daggers, flasks, writing materials, and perfume. There were umbrellas with windows and with tiny sponges to catch drips. There was even one umbrella that whistled when it was opened. But for the most part, umbrellas remained plain and practical.

Not so parasols—new fashions in women's parasols were introduced every year. Handles were made of porcelain, ivory, jade, and rare woods and were sometimes set with precious stones. Covers were made of silk and other expensive fabrics, often lined in a contrasting color and trimmed with ribbons, feathers, and lace. A more practical design was adopted by Queen Victoria, who had several of her parasols lined with chain mail after someone tried to shoot her.

Until the 1920's, no well-dressed woman's wardrobe was complete without a parasol in the latest style. Then the parasol was replaced by another fashion—the suntan. But umbrellas remained popular. And, meanwhile, superstitions had grown up around them. Many people believed it was unlucky to open an umbrella indoors. Some people believed it was unlucky to lay a folded umbrella on a bed or even on a table.

Umbrellas seemed to have other magical powers, too—for example, the power to affect the weather. People said that if you left your umbrella home, it was sure to rain, while if you carried it, the sun would surely shine. Umbrellas also seemed to have a remarkable talent for disappearing. They were left behind in public places, carried off by strangers by mistake, lent to friends and not returned, and just plain stolen. This talent gave rise to the following rhyme:

> The rain it raineth on the just
>   And also on the unjust fella;
> But chiefly on the just, because
>   The unjust steals the just's umbrella.

Umbrellas have also figured in literature. In Daniel Defoe's *Robinson Crusoe,* the castaway with great difficulty fashions an umbrella from animal skins, for protection from both heat and rain. Robinson Crusoe became so closely associated with his um-

Mary Poppins, "floating away over the cherry trees and the roofs of the houses, holding tightly to the umbrella."

brella that for a time umbrellas were called Robinsons. Later they were nicknamed gamps, after a character in Charles Dickens' *Martin Chuzzlewit.* (Mrs. Gamp is a nurse who carries a battered, loosely rolled umbrella.) And one of the best-loved characters in children's literature, Mary Poppins, is seldom without her umbrella. At the end of P. L. Travers' book *Mary Poppins,* she steps outside, snaps open her umbrella, and sails off into the sky.

SNOW MONKEYS OF JAPAN

Most monkeys live in warm lands. But the Japanese macaque (muh-KAK) is a monkey that lives high in the mountains of Japan, where the winters are cold and snowy. For this reason, the Japanese macaque has another name—the snow monkey.

Snow monkeys are large, strong animals. The males, which are bigger than the females, may weigh as much as 40 pounds (18 kilograms). Most have pale gray or brown fur, with pink skin on the face and rump. They don't have a very good sense of smell. But they have excellent vision and very good hearing.

Several features help snow monkeys survive the icy winters. Their fur is much thicker and longer than the fur of monkeys that live in warmer lands. They have short, stumpy tails—so not as much heat is lost to the air as would be from a long tail. And since the monkeys spend most of their time on the ground, they don't need long tails to help them hold onto tree branches. At night, as they sleep, the snow monkeys keep warm by huddling close together or curling up into balls.

Snow monkeys have long, sharp teeth. They eat fruit, leaves, grain, and insects. In winter, they dig through snow drifts in search of grass. They also eat the needles of evergreen trees. And if nothing else is available, they will even eat the bark of trees.

Snow monkeys are very social animals, and they live in groups called troops. A troop usually has 30 to 150 members. Each troop has its own territory.

Adult males act as leaders and guards. They watch for danger, screeching loudly and waving their arms when they spot an enemy or an intruder. They also decide where the troop will move. Different parts of the territory are visited at different times of the year, to take advantage of ripening fruit and other changes in food supplies.

When the troop moves around its territory, some males go first while others bring up the rear. In between are the females and children. When the troop stops to feed, two circles are formed, one within the other. The central circle consists mainly of the females and young monkeys. The outer circle consists of adult males.

In winter, a day's outing will often include a stop at a hot spring. The snow monkeys like to bathe in the warm water. It's a pleasant way to escape from the chilly air and the snow-covered ground.

Babies are born in the spring, after the snow has melted. They are very tiny and weigh less than a pound (0.5 kilogram). Snow monkeys don't have nests or dens. So when the troop travels, the babies must travel too. At first, the mother clasps the baby against her breast while she travels along on three legs. When the baby gets bigger, it rides on the mother's back.

Snow monkeys are quick learners. Remember the saying "monkey see, monkey do"? One Japanese scientist found proof that this is often a true statement. He was studying a troop of Japanese macaques on the small, mountainous island of Koshima. He and his fellow researchers gave names to a few of the macaques. They named one female Imo. She was about 18 months old.

One day, Imo picked up a sweet potato that was covered with sand. She put the potato in water, then rubbed off the sand with her hands. To everyone's knowledge, no other macaque had ever done such a thing.

About a month later, one of Imo's friends started to wash sweet potatoes before eating them. After several more months, Imo's mother was doing the same thing. Gradually, this behavior spread through the troop. After ten years, 42 of the 59 members of the troop had adopted the habit. Those who hadn't were older monkeys—ones who were already adults when Imo made her discovery.

A snow-covered Japanese macaque warms up by taking a leisurely bath in a hot spring on a cold winter day.

Like some people, the older monkeys had apparently become too set in their habits to try new ways of doing things.

When Imo was 4 years old, she made another discovery. Sometimes the researchers put grains of wheat on the beach for the macaques. You can imagine how hard it would be to eat the wheat without getting sand in your mouth. Imo threw a handful of sand and wheat into the water. The sand sank to the bottom. The wheat, which is very light in weight, floated to the surface. This made it easy for Imo to gather and eat clean grains. Other macaques observed this and soon began copying Imo.

The Japanese are very fond of snow monkeys. They have written stories about them, and artists often paint them. You may have seen a statue or a drawing of three monkeys in which one monkey is covering its eyes, a second is holding its ears, and the third is covering its mouth. These are snow monkeys, and they represent the famous saying of Buddha: "See no evil, hear no evil, speak no evil."

JENNY TESAR
Series Consultant
Wonders of Wildlife

WATER LILIES

Imagine discovering a floating garden filled with colorful flowers atop clusters of round, green leaves. A frog basks happily in the sun on a leaf it uses as a small raft. Fish weave patterns beneath the leaves. Dragonflies dart from blossom to blossom. You might not think of a shallow lake or a slow-flowing stream as a garden, but these are the habitats of water lilies—some of nature's most beautiful creations.

Water lilies come in many sizes and colors and are found in many parts of the world. There is a great variety of wild species, and many others are hybrids that have been specially cultivated by botanists. Despite their name, water lilies are not members of the lily family. They belong to the family *Nymphaeaceae*. Long ago, before scientists had classified all the plants, "lily" was used to describe any especially beautiful flower. And that is how water lilies were given their popular name.

HOW THEY GROW

Although they live in water, water lilies have the same basic parts as flowering land plants. Most species of water lily grow from a thick underground stem buried in the mud bottom of a pond, lake, or stream. The stem produces roots that grow down into the mud. And it sends long, flexible stalks up through the water. Some stalks support leaves; other stalks support flowers.

The leaves are large, flat, and nearly circular. They are often called lily pads. Usually the leaves float on the surface of the water, but in some species they are slightly beneath the surface.

Water lily flowers are many-petaled. They come in a multitude of colors—white, yellow, pink, blue, apricot, purple, even green. They may be as large as dinner plates or as small as your thumb nail. Supported by their stalks, the flowers float or rise somewhat above the surface of the water.

Each plant produces only one flower at a time, and the flower lives about three days. But one plant may continue to blossom throughout the course of the growing season. Some water lily plants bear more than 100 blooms a year. In tropical lands, water lily flowers can be seen all year round. In cooler climates, they blossom from early spring until the first frosts of autumn.

Some water lilies bloom during the day, then close up as darkness falls. Others are night bloomers, opening their petals only after the sun has passed beyond the horizon. At one time, night-blooming varieties were called husband lilies—because they opened as the man of the house returned home from work.

There are a great many varieties of water lilies, and they are found in many parts of the world. The large, flat leaves are sometimes variegated in color. The flowers come in every shade of the rainbow. They either float on the leaves or rise above the surface of the water.

49

The leaves of the royal water lily look like enormous pie plates. They are strong enough to support a child. And the flowers are pollinated in a most unusual way.

The purpose of the flowers is to attract insects, which pollinate the flowers. Pollination of water lilies takes place when pollen from the male part of one flower is transferred to the female part of another flower. Pollination is necessary for the formation of seeds.

Many water lilies use their colorful petals to attract insects. Some species smell sweet, and they depend on their scent to lure insects. Beetles, flies, and other insects crowd around for a free lunch. They feed on nectar, a juice produced by the flower. As the insects crawl over the flowers, pollen sticks to their bodies. Later, when they crawl over other flowers, they leave behind the pollen picked up from the water lilies they visited earlier.

After the flowers have been pollinated, and when they finish blooming, they close up like buds and sink to the bottom of the water. There, they produce seeds, which will eventually grow into new water lily plants.

ROYAL WATER LILIES

Perhaps the most spectacular water lily is a giant species called the royal water lily. The plant's scientific name is *Victoria amazonica,* and it is a native of the Amazon River basin of South America. It was named in honor of Queen Victoria, the 19th-century ruler of Britain.

The leaves of the royal water lily look like enormous pie plates. They may be seven feet (2 meters) in diameter. The leaves have upturned edges that prevent water from getting on top. A network of narrow ribs crisscrosses the underside of each leaf. The ribs make the huge leaves so strong that they can support the weight of a child. In Peru, Indian mothers sometimes left their babies on the leaves while they gathered water lily seeds. One bird—the jacana, or lily trotter—often builds its nest and raises its young on these leaves.

The flowers of the royal water lily may be a foot (30 centimeters) or more in diameter. They open on two successive nights. On the first night, the flowers are creamy white. By the second night they have changed to a reddish purple. But the flowers have done more than change color. They have also been pollinated. And this they have achieved in a most unusual way.

When the flowers first open, they have a strong, fruity odor. The smell is said to resemble a mixture of pineapple and butterscotch. This strong scent attracts large scarab beetles. In the dark of night, the beetles crawl deep into the flower in search of nectar. Toward morning, the scent slowly disappears. The flower closes, trapping the beetles inside. The flower stays closed all day long. By the time it reopens the next evening, the captured beetles are eager to escape. They are all covered with a sticky substance produced by the flower. And as they leave the flower, they cannot help but become dusted with pollen. They fly off, in search of white, sweet-smelling flowers. And as they crawl into the newly opened blossoms, they deposit the pollen from the flowers that had trapped them the night before.

SACRED FLOWERS

During times of drought, a lake bed may dry up. The water lilies seem to completely disappear. But the roots and stems buried in the mud survive. When the rains return, new leaves begin to grow, and soon the water is filled with lily pads and colorful flowers.

Ancient peoples witnessed the return of the water lilies, and they believed that the plants were sacred. They saw water lilies as symbols of immortality—the ability to live forever. And they considered water lilies to be symbols of resurrection—the ability to return to life after death.

The favorite sacred plant of the ancient Egyptians was a night-blooming water lily called the lotus flower (*Nymphaea lotus*). It was the flower of Isis, the goddess of motherhood. The Egyptians often decorated their buildings with drawings and sculptures of lotus flowers. They also made coins decorated with these flowers. When an important Egyptian nobleman entertained, his guests were given lotus flowers. The guests held the blossoms or wore them in their hair.

The lotus also played an important role in funerals. Petals of lotus flowers have been found in ancient graves. They were found in the funeral wreath of Ramses II, an Egyptian ruler who died more than 3,000 years ago.

In China and India, people worshipped the sacred lotus (*Nelumbo nucifera*). The large but delicate pink flowers of this plant are on stalks that rise several feet out of the water. The people believed that their gods sat in the center of these lotus blossoms.

The seed container of the sacred lotus is very attractive. It is bowl-shaped, with a flat top. The top is pierced with holes, and in the holes are the seeds. Birds pick the seeds out of the holes. Many are dropped by the birds as they fly. If the seeds fall into water, they sink to the bottom. And some of the seeds will grow into new plants.

USES PAST AND PRESENT

Throughout history, water lilies have served several purposes. In Ireland and Scotland, people made a blue-black dye from the roots of the plants. They used the dye to color wool.

Various parts of water lily plants have been used to treat illnesses, although there is no scientific proof that such medicines really work. The powdered roots of one kind of water lily have been used to treat digestive problems. The leaves of another are said to be good for curing fevers. And, said one writer, "The syrup of the flowers produces rest and settles the brain of frantic persons."

Every part of a water lily plant can be eaten. In China, people eat the stem, either raw or cooked. They wrap fresh water lily leaves around meat, and then steam the combination. In South America the seeds are ground to make flour, which is used to make a delicious pastry. The ancient Egyptians also made flour from water lily seeds, then used the flour to make bread.

Today water lilies are appreciated chiefly for their beauty. Many people plant them in ponds or even in small tubs. Special aquatic nurseries can advise you on getting the correct balance of plants and water creatures, and you can create your own floating garden.

The seed pod of the sacred lotus is pierced with holes containing the seeds. In China and India, the people believed their gods sat in the center of the blossoms.

YARN THINGS

These attractive items—all made with yarn—can be used as coasters, key rings, or ornaments. And they are easy to make. First, buy plastic mesh forms, which are available in craft stores. They come in various shapes: round, square, diamond, and six-sided. Embroider a design on the mesh, using two or three different colors of yarn. When you have finished, put the object on a piece of felt and trace around it. (The felt should match one of the yarn colors.) Cut out the felt. Using white glue, neatly attach the felt to the back of the object.

SASSY SOAPS

Soaps come in many attractive shapes and colors. You can make them even more attractive by personalizing them. In only a few minutes you can create one-of-a-kind soaps that will delight your friends and family.

First, gather several bars of soap that you would like to decorate. The bars don't have to be new; they can be partially used. If the bars have nicks or scratches, wet them and gently rub the marks until they disappear.

Now find some pictures that you think would look nice on the soaps. The pictures can be found in magazines and newspapers. They can be cut from greeting cards and gift wrap. They can be photographs, stamps, or decals. You can even draw your own pictures and designs.

Cut out each picture so that it will fit on one side of the soap. If the soap has a name or other information etched into it, choose a picture that's large enough to cover the writing. After you have decided how you want to position the picture, use paste or white glue to attach it to the soap.

To prevent the picture from fading or washing away, it must be sealed to the soap. Clear nail polish can be used as the sealer. Cover the picture with a thin coat of polish —you should extend the polish onto the soap, about one inch (2.5 centimeters) beyond the edge of the picture. Let the nail polish dry thoroughly. Then apply a second coat.

Decorated soaps make wonderful presents. Choose decorations that will please the person to whom you will give the soaps. Teenagers might like soaps decorated with pictures of their favorite rock stars or animals. People who like to garden may enjoy soaps covered with pictures of flowers. A jogger might like them decorated with pictures of sneakers.

Soaps can also be decorated to match the room in which they will be used. Or they can be decorated with holiday pictures—hearts for Valentine's Day, a turkey for Thanksgiving. The possibilities are as varied as your imagination.

Punch and Judy is the most famous of all puppet plays.

TALES TOLD BY PUPPETS

Ladies and Gentlemen, pray how you do?
If you all happy, me all happy too.
Stop and hear my merry littel play;
If me make you laugh, me need not make you pay.

These words begin one version of the most famous of all puppet plays, *Punch and Judy*. They are spoken by Punch, a mischievous hand-puppet character with a long hooked nose and a high squeaky voice. As the play begins, Punch is singing and dancing. When his neighbor's dog, Toby, comes onto the stage, Punch tries to be friendly. But Toby bites Punch on the nose. "Oh my nose! my pretty littel nose!" cries Punch.

Toby is the first of many opponents that Punch faces. He fights with his servant, his landlord, a doctor, a judge, his child—even with his wife (Judy). In most encounters, Punch emerges victorious—often because he kills his opponent. Finally, a policeman arrives and drags the outrageous but comical Punch off to jail.

Jack Ketch, the hangman, sets up the gallows. It looks like the end for Punch. But Punch tricks Jack Ketch and talks him into putting his own head in the noose!

As the play ends, Punch is singing and dancing—and once again whacking his way through life with a stick. And the people who watched his "merry littel play" are filled with laughter.

Puppet plays are one of the oldest forms of entertainment. They have been performed for thousands of years all over the world. The *Punch and Judy* we know today is English in origin. But each culture has developed its own special puppet heroes and heroines, often drawn from the folktales of the time. Many of today's most popular puppet shows are hundreds of years old. Punch shows—and there are many versions in many countries—have been performed for more than 300 years. Even older is Orlando, the hero of an epic tale from Sicily.

THE ADVENTURES OF ORLANDO
The character of Orlando was originally based on Roland, a knight who lived in medieval times. Roland was commander of Charlemagne's rear guard when Charlemagne and his army returned to France in A.D. 778. As the army traveled through the mountains between Spain and France, ene-

mies separated the rear guard from the rest of the army. Roland died in the fighting.

So much is true. But the puppet tales of Orlando have become colorful and exciting mixtures of history, legend, and fantasy. In one adventure, the girl that Orlando loves marries someone else. Orlando goes mad. That is, he loses his wits. His wits are taken to the moon, where they are kept in an urn. The good knight Astolfo goes to the moon to recover Orlando's wits and carries them back to earth. Then he ties up the mad Orlando and holds the urn up to Orlando's nose. The wits leave the urn and enter Orlando's head through his nose, and Orlando is sane again.

In another tale, Orlando's cousin Rinaldo mistakenly drinks from the fountain of hate, while the girl he loves drinks from the fountain of love. Much confusion results.

There are numerous battles, too. The knights commanded by Orlando are dressed in shining armor. They are skilled sword fighters who are eventually victorious over their enemies. But sometimes blood, in the form of beet juice, is shed.

There are more than 250 Orlando puppet plays, each one with numerous adventures. They are usually performed in a serial fashion every night. Sometimes it takes six months to see the entire story. There are also lots of characters—about 50, not counting women, foot soldiers, devils, dragons, angels, and witches. In a well-done battle, 40 main characters may be on stage. The puppeteers must remember which ones die . . . and be sure that those appearing in the following night's tale remain alive.

The wooden marionettes (puppets moved from above) used in the Orlando epic are almost life size. They are also very heavy—especially if they are wearing armor. They are controlled by iron rods, and, as you can imagine, it takes a lot of strength to work these puppets.

CHINESE PUPPET PLAYS

In China, the stars of many puppet plays are females. In one play, a shepherd tells about a fierce tiger that lives on the mountain and claims that he has no fear of it. When the tiger actually appears, the shepherd thinks it's a pussy cat. A voice warns him that the animal is a tiger. The shepherd runs off to get a spear, and then pokes the tiger in the nose with it. Suddenly the tiger jumps up and swallows the shepherd whole.

When the shepherd's wife comes looking for her husband, she discovers the tiger. A voice tells her that the tiger has eaten her

The wooden marionettes used in the Orlando adventures are almost life size, and they are controlled by iron rods.

husband. The woman seizes the spear and kills the tiger. Then she reaches into the tiger's mouth and pulls out her husband. She gives him a good scolding—and insists that he carry her home. The tale of the shepherd, like *Punch and Judy,* is told with hand puppets. (The puppet is worn over the hand like a glove.)

Also popular in China are shadow puppets. (Shadows of the puppets are cast on a screen by a light from behind.) One story told with shadow puppets concerns an emperor named Wu Ti. When a girl he loves dies, Wu Ti becomes very depressed. His sadness is so enormous that he is unable to work. Wu Ti's friends are worried, so they offer a reward to anyone who can cure Wu Ti's depression.

A clever magician hears of the reward. He makes an image of the girl, which he shows against a light screen in Wu Ti's palace. The figure looks exactly like the girl who died. It even moves and speaks like the girl. Wu Ti is convinced that it *is* the girl. His depression is cured, and he is able to return to work.

BURMESE PUPPET PLAYS

In Burma, marionettes are used to tell the 550 birth stories of the Buddha. The Buddha, who lived in India from 563 to 483 B.C., was the founder of Buddhism, one of the world's great religions.

One traditional marionette show in Burma uses more than twenty puppets. Among them are a horse, two elephants (one white, one black), a tiger, a monkey, a king, an astrologer, a hermit, and two clowns. The good characters, such as kings and elephants, enter from the right side of the stage. Evil characters, such as tigers, enter from the left.

A Burmese puppet play may last all night. The first part of a traditional play may tell about the creation of the world. Animals play an important role in this. The second part is about humans on earth.

GREEK AND TURKISH PUPPET PLAYS

The main characters in puppet theaters in Greece and Turkey were modeled hundreds of years ago after two Turkish workers. Legend has it that Karagoz, a mason, and Hacivad, a blacksmith, were helping to build a mosque for the sultan. They were natural comedians and were always clowning around. This distracted the other workers, and as a result little if any progress was made on the mosque. When the sultan heard this, he was furious. He ordered the immediate execution of Karagoz and Hacivad. But after their deaths, the sultan regretted his action.

A courtier named Sheik Kusteri wanted to cheer the ruler. He made shadow puppets of Karagoz and Hacivad and cleverly imitated their behavior. The play delighted the sultan.

Some of the most famous puppet shows take their heroes and heroines from stories written for young people—such as *Alice in Wonderland*.

Over the centuries, more and more puppet plays were written about Karagoz and Hacivad, and the cast of characters grew too. The stories were usually very involved and funny. Karagoz and Hacivad had many arguments, which sooner or later ended in fights. It was easy to tell the two shadow puppets apart. Karagoz had a rounded beard while Hacivad's beard was pointed. The two men also had different personalities.

Hacivad had a very high opinion of himself and thought he was very intelligent. Karagoz was a simple gypsy who was often the target of other people's jokes. But like Punch, he had no respect for authority and was able to take care of himself. He would poke fun at lawyers, landlords, and minor government officials. At least, Karagoz would do this when he performed before an audience of working people. When the puppet performed in the sultan's palace, he was much better behaved.

PUPPETS IN THE AMERICAS

Puppets have always been popular in the Americas. In early times, American Indians often used puppets in religious ceremonies. For example, the Hopi used six large snake puppets in their corn ceremony. In another ceremony, the Hopi used marionettes of girls grinding corn. As the puppets knelt on the ground, moving back and forth over the grinding stone, the audience believed they were watching real girls.

As in many cultures, puppet shows in North America today often take their heroes and heroines from folk and fairy tales, such as *Robin Hood, Cinderella,* and *Rip Van Winkle.* Other puppet shows are based on literature, especially stories that were written for young people—*Alice in Wonderland, Treasure Island,* and *Pinocchio.*

And while the history of puppetry is old, new chapters are still being written. In recent decades new puppet heroes and heroines have been born: Howdy Doody, Charlemane the Lion, Kukla and Ollie, Miss Piggy, Kermit the Frog. Like their ancestors, they tell their tales and create a magical world for people of all ages.

Reviewed by BIL BAIRD
Puppeteer and Author

Grandma's Helpless Helpers

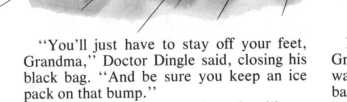

"You'll just have to stay off your feet, Grandma," Doctor Dingle said, closing his black bag. "And be sure you keep an ice pack on that bump."

"I can't just lie here on the sofa with my feet propped up on a pillow," Grandma Duck answered. "This is a farm! I've got chores."

Doctor Dingle shook his head.

"No chores for you, Grandma. You took a nasty fall, and I want you to rest all day."

Doctor Dingle put on his overcoat, picked up his black bag, and walked to the front door.

"Why don't you call your nephew and see if he can help you out today?" he suggested.

Doctor Dingle closed the door behind him. Grandma heard his car drive away.

"A fine kettle of fish!" Grandma grumbled to herself.

It had happened that very morning. Grandma had hopped out of bed, as she always did, dressed, and headed out to the barn to milk the cows. About halfway to the barn, a jackrabbit had sprinted across her path. The next thing she knew, she was sitting on the ground with a very painful bump on her forehead.

And now she was flat on her back, an ice pack on her head, with orders to stay off her feet for the rest of the day.

"A fine kettle of fish!" Grandma grumbled a second time. But she couldn't escape the fact that she needed help.

Grandma reached for the telephone and dialed Donald's number. An hour later, Donald and his nephews burst in.

"Don't worry about a thing, Grandma," Donald said. "We can take care of all your chores, can't we, boys?"

"You bet, Grandma!" Huey answered. "Just leave everything to us."

"Tell us what to do and it's as good as done!" Louie added.

"Thanks, boys," Grandma said. "I've made a list of everything." She handed it to Donald.

"Wow!" Donald said. "That's quite a list."

"There's always plenty to do on a farm," Grandma answered. "Now let me explain some of these chores . . ."

"Tut-tut, Grandma," said Donald, holding up his hand. "We're not your relatives for nothing. We can handle it."

Grandma watched Donald and the boys rush away, full of enthusiasm. She wondered if calling Donald had been the right thing to do. But what else could she have done?

Outside, Donald assigned the chores. "You milk the cows, Huey. Dewey will feed the chickens and gather the eggs."

"What should I do?" Louie asked.

"You'll help me fix Grandma's roof!"

Huey and Dewey ran off toward the barn and the chicken coop.

"Now, then, let's see if we can find a ladder," Donald said to Louie.

Huey was the first to arrive at his assigned job. He unlatched the barn door. The inside of the barn was dark, and it took Huey a few minutes to see the three cows who were munching hay in their stalls.

The cows looked at Huey and Huey looked at the cows. Of course, Huey had seen cows before. And once or twice, he had watched Grandma milk them. But doing it himself was quite another matter.

First of all, he remembered, he needed a milk pail. It was so dark in the barn, he could hardly see anything, so Huey opened

the door to let in more light. At the back of the barn, hanging on a nail, was a bucket.

Huey walked to the rear of the barn and took down the pail. When he turned back, he couldn't believe his eyes. The cows were gone!

Meanwhile, Dewey was having a problem, too. He couldn't find the chicken feed. Or, to put it more correctly, he didn't know what chicken feed looked like. He found a sack of something, but he didn't know if it was the right stuff.

"I'd better go ask Grandma," he thought.

He picked up the bag and headed for the farmhouse. He didn't notice there was a hole in the bottom of the bag. But the chickens did. Dewey walked toward the house, leaving a trail of chicken feed behind him. Naturally, the chickens followed the tasty trail.

At the same time, up on the farmhouse roof, Donald and Louie were tackling the repair.

"Are you sure you know how to do this, Uncle Donald?" Louie asked.

"Trust me," Donald said, stepping toward a particularly fragile-looking part of the roof.

Grandma was snoozing comfortably on the sofa when she heard the first "Moo!"

For a moment, she thought she had dreamed it. But when she opened her eyes and saw three cows standing in her living room, she knew it was too crazy to be a dream.

"Awk!" was all she could manage to say.

Just then, Dewey marched in carrying a leaking sack of chicken feed, and followed by sixteen chickens!

Next came Huey. "So that's where you went!" he said to his vanishing cows. The cows had wandered out through the barn door Huey had left open, and into Grandma's house through the back door Louie had forgotten to close.

Now there were cows and chickens wandering through Grandma's house, mooing and clucking, while Huey and Dewey desperately tried to get them back outside where they belonged.

"What next?" Grandma moaned.

As if in answer to her question, there was a loud cracking noise overhead.

Grandma, Huey, Dewey, three cows, and sixteen chickens looked up just in time to

see Donald come crashing through the ceiling in a shower of shingles. With a thud, he landed in Grandma's big stuffed chair.

"Uh . . . hi, Grandma," said Donald, raising a limp hand.

Grandma Duck sat straight up on the sofa. "I can see that my farm chores are just too much for you city boys to handle," she began.

"Oh, Grandma—no!" chorused Huey, Dewey, and Louie.

"We came here to help you, Grandma," added Donald. "Please give us another chance."

Grandma looked from one sorry face to another, and decided that they might have learned a lesson.

So she explained to Huey very carefully, in great detail, how to milk a cow properly. With some help from his brothers, Huey shoved the cows out of the house and back to the barn.

Then Grandma told Dewey where to find another sack of chicken feed. When Dewey went to get it, the hens followed him out the door and right back to their coop, where no one was going to come crashing down on them through the roof.

"Now, Donald," began Grandma.

"I know, Grandma," said Donald. "We're going to be careful where we step. Don't worry." And he and Louie went out to repair the roof.

Grandma lay back on the sofa and put the ice pack on her forehead. "Don't worry," she mumbled to herself. "We'll see . . ."

But everyone was pleasantly surprised by how easily everything got done. Huey bribed his cows with big handfuls of sweet pink clover, and the milking got done without incident. Dewey's hens didn't even squawk when he gently lifted each one off her nest to collect her egg. And working together, Donald and Louie soon made Grandma's roof as good as new.

The rest of the chores went quickly, with the help of a little good advice from Grandma. Late that afternoon, Dewey piped up to ask, "Gee, Grandma, isn't there anything else we can do to help you?"

"I think there's only one thing left," twinkled Grandma. "It's something I can't let go any longer."

Donald and the boys looked at one another. They were bone tired from working around the farm all day, but, after all, they had come out here to help their Grandma.

Donald smiled weakly at her. "Sure, Grandma," he said, thinking that the well pump probably needed repair, or maybe the tractor needed an overhaul. "What is it?"

Grandma laughed out loud. She could tell from his face what Donald had been thinking. "Go out to the kitchen and cut us each a big slice of that plum pie," she chuckled. "You 'farmhands' have earned it!"

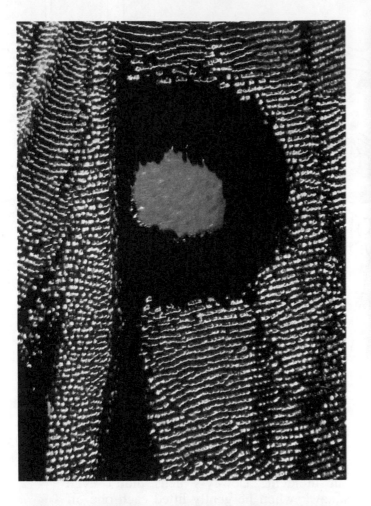

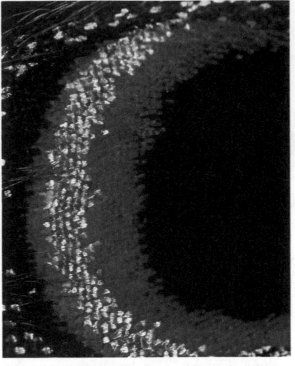

"A" IS FOR BUTTERFLY

If you look carefully, you will find common things in uncommon places. The letters of the alphabet, for instance, are usually found in books, newspapers, and magazines. But the letters shown on these pages were found in the colorful wing patterns of butterflies and moths. Thousands of people probably looked at the insects without seeing the letters. Perhaps you were one of them. But a

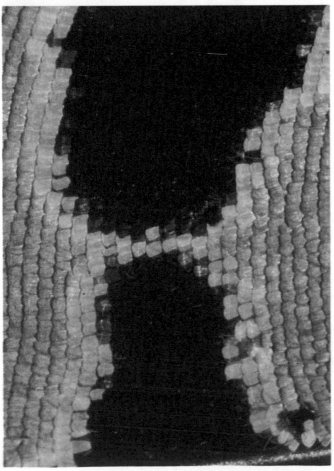

photographer with a sharp eye and an imaginative mind saw and snapped the letters.

Imagine what else might be seen in the wings of insects, the bark of trees, or a cloud-filled sky. Open up your mind, put film in your camera, and look for the usual in unusual places. At first you may want to photograph everything that is out of the ordinary. Later you may wish to specialize in one particular subject or in one type of pattern. This is a hobby that will give you pleasure for a long time.

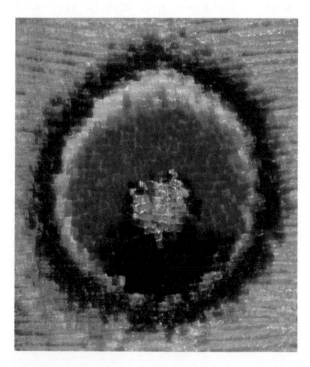

SKY SPECTACLES

Without the air around us and the sun above us, the earth would be a very different place. The sky would look black. There would be no winds, no clouds, no rain. You wouldn't ever see a sunset or a rainbow or lightning.

The blanket of air surrounding the earth is called the atmosphere. It is made up of tiny molecules of gases, water vapor, and dust particles. The sun is a great ball of hot gases. The light that it gives off is called white light. But it is really made up of all seven colors of the spectrum—violet, indigo, blue, green, yellow, orange, and red. As the sun's white light passes through the atmosphere, it is split up and scattered—spreading light and color into a sky that would otherwise be dark.

But sunlight passes through an atmosphere that is contantly changing. Winds form. Water vapor condenses around dust particles. Clouds and rain occur. It is these and other changes that produce the dramatic sky spectacles you see on these pages.

Rainbows. A rainbow is a brilliant arc of colors in the sky. Rainbows appear after a rainstorm when there is a great amount of moisture in the air and the sun is shining brightly. Rainbows may also be seen when sunlight hits a waterfall, a fountain, or even the spray from a garden hose.

A rainbow is simply sunlight that has been refracted (bent) by water. As rays of sunlight pass through a droplet of water in the air, the water acts like a prism. It splits up the light into seven colors. Each colored ray is bent and leaves the drop at a different angle. When sunlight strikes billions of droplets, arching bands of color are formed. Every rainbow contains all seven colors. You don't see them all because the colors blend into each other.

A rainbow is really a complete circle. We usually see only part of it because the bottom half lies below the horizon and is thus hidden

from view. You can see the complete circle of a rainbow from an airplane because there is no horizon to cut off the view.

Halos. During the winter you may see a halo—a ring of light—around the sun or moon. A halo occurs when moonlight or sunlight shines through tiny ice crystals in the earth's upper atmosphere. The crystals bend the light much as water drops bend light to form rainbows.

To the unaided eye, some halos may appear as white light. Halos are sometimes even called "white rainbows." But even though we may not see them, a halo actually contains all the colors of the spectrum.

Lightning. Lightning is a huge spark of electricity. When storm clouds form, particles in the clouds develop positive and negative electrical charges. Suddenly a spark of electricity jumps from a group of negative particles to a nearby group of positive particles. This sets off a chain reaction that produces a lightning flash. We don't see the particles. We see air that has been made to glow by the passage of these charged particles.

Lightning takes place within a cloud, between two clouds, or between a cloud and the ground. Lightning seldom travels in a straight line. It zigzags and branches as the electricity seeks the easiest path between negative and positive particles.

Sunsets and Sunrises. As the sun's light passes through the atmosphere, the blue and

violet parts are usually more scattered than any of the other colors. And so we have a blue sky for much of the day. But during sunset and sunrise, when the sun is close to the horizon, brilliant reds, pinks, and oranges may color the sky.

This occurs because there is a denser concentration of dust and water particles in the lower atmosphere. When the sun is near the horizon and shines through this denser concentration, the shorter wavelengths of light —violets, blues, and greens—are absorbed. Only the longer wavelengths—reds and oranges—come through directly, so the sun, clouds, and sky appear reddish.

Lewis Carroll

Louisa May Alcott

A. A. Milne

HAPPY BIRTHDAY,

from Alice, Jo, & Pooh

The anniversaries of the births of three famous writers were celebrated in 1982—Lewis Carroll, Louisa May Alcott, and A. A. Milne. Carroll and Alcott had been born 150 years earlier; Milne, 100.

All three wrote works for adults that are now for the most part forgotten. But it was their books for young people that made these writers famous in their own time and beloved ever since. Carroll was the creator of Alice, whose dreamlike adventures in Wonderland have charmed millions of readers. Alcott created the March sisters, the "little women" of her famous novel. And Milne invented the lovable bear Winnie-the-Pooh.

LEWIS CARROLL (1832–1898)

Lewis Carroll was the pen name of the Rev. Charles Lutwidge Dodgson, who was born on January 27, 1832, in western England. He was a don—a faculty member—at Oxford University, where he taught mathematics. Dodgson never married and had few close family ties. But he was a man of many interests. He was a skillful and enthusiastic amateur photographer (and photography was a new—and complicated—thing then). He took an interest in university politics and wrote satires on various questions that arose in his college, Christ Church. He wrote books on mathematics and on logic. And he devised games and invented gadgets. But

Dodgson is chiefly remembered today for the books he wrote for young people.

In 1856, Dodgson met the child who inspired his most famous books. Alice Liddell (rhymes with fiddle) was the daughter of the dean of Christ Church. She and her sisters, Lorina and Edith, soon became good friends of the shy mathematics lecturer.

On July 4, 1862, Dodgson and another don, the Rev. Robinson Duckworth, took the Liddell girls on a picnic. As they rowed up the river, 10-year-old Alice asked Dodgson to tell them a story. He had often done so, but this time he seemed particularly inspired. When they got home, Alice begged him to write the story out for her. He did. In

1864, as a Christmas gift, he presented her with a book, hand-written and illustrated by him. He called it *Alice's Adventures Under Ground.*

Meanwhile, Dodgson had shown the story to several friends, who encouraged him to publish it. He expanded the original story and chose John Tenniel, a well-known illustrator, to do the pictures. *Alice's Adventures in Wonderland* soon appeared—the first book published under the pen name Lewis Carroll. It was followed a few years later by a sequel, *Through the Looking-Glass and What Alice Found There.*

Dodgson wrote other books under the pen name Lewis Carroll, along with booklets giving instructions for games he had invented, a few essays, books of verse, and *A Tangled Tale,* a series of stories containing some knotty mathematical puzzles. And he wrote many letters sprinkled with puns, puzzles, acrostics, and nonsense. Some of these have been published.

The Books. *Alice's Adventures in Wonderland* (1865) and *Through the Looking-Glass* (1872) recount the dream adventures of a little English girl named Alice, who is as sensible a girl as you could hope to meet. The charm of the books lies in the way they combine fantasy and nonsense with mathematical logic that is carried to extremes. They are filled with parody and puns. In the first book, Alice follows a white rabbit (who wears gloves and carries a fan) down a rabbit hole. In the wonderland at the bottom, she has fantastic adventures—she grows larger and smaller as she eats and drinks things, she plays croquet using a flamingo for a mallet, and she takes part in the maddeningly unfair trial of the Knave of Hearts. And she meets some strange and unforgettable characters— the Cheshire Cat, the Mad Hatter, the Mock Turtle, the King and Queen of Hearts.

In *Through the Looking-Glass,* Alice goes through her living-room mirror. Her adventures on the other side are tied together by two themes. One is a chess game (the book may have been inspired by the young Liddells' learning chess), in which Alice takes the part of a white pawn. The other is that

Left: Alice meets the Cheshire Cat in *Alice's Adventures in Wonderland.*
Right: The Walrus and the Carpenter appear in *Through the Looking-Glass.*

The Wonderland Postage-Stamp Case

M.A.A.D. from C.L.D. Mar. 1890.

WONDERFUL INVENTIONS

Charles Lutwidge Dodgson was much more than a writer. Among other things, he was a talented inventor. One of his inventions, for example, was a device he called the Nyctograph. It allowed him to record his nighttime thoughts in Braille-like symbols—without getting out of bed.

Dodgson also created puzzles, games, and gadgets. The Wonderland Postage-Stamp Case, which he designed, was a clever and convenient way to store a supply of stamps. The cover (*left*) shows Alice holding the Duchess's baby. But in the picture on the case inside (*center*), the baby has changed into a pig—just as it does in *Alice's Adventures in Wonderland.* The back of the case shows the Cheshire Cat, which gradually fades away until only its wide grin remains.

everything is backwards—people have to run to stay in place, and Alice is offered a dry biscuit to quench her thirst. As in the first book, Alice is resourceful and intelligent in the face of her bewildering adventures. The lasting popularity of the two books may stem in part from the fact that many children, confronted with a confusing adult world, feel a bit like Alice.

The Hunting of the Snark (1876) is a narrative poem. It tells of the expedition of the Bellman and his odd crew—their occupations all begin with the letter B—to hunt the Snark:

They sought it with thimbles, they sought it
   with care;
They pursued it with forks and hope;
They threatened its life with a railway-share;
They charmed it with smiles and soap.

Critics tried to find some deep meanings in this inspired nonsense, and Carroll said they were welcome to try. He had certainly intended none, he wrote, but "words mean more than we mean to express when we use them."

Sylvie and Bruno (1889) and *Sylvie and Bruno Concluded* (1893) have never been as popular as Carroll's other books. That may be because they are a blend of two quite different stories. In both books, the narrator recounts two sets of events, which he observes and takes part in, switching from one to the other. One set is a serious, grown-up story of a young lady's courtship by two suitors. The characters discuss such sober matters as charity bazaars, how to keep Sunday, and the problem of the idle rich. The other set of events is pure fantasy. It deals with the fairy children Sylvie and Bruno, their friend the Professor, their wicked uncle, and their father, who becomes king of Elfland.

LOUISA MAY ALCOTT (1832–1888)

Louisa May Alcott wrote things from the time she was a child—a diary, poems and stories, and plays that she and her three sisters put on. But it was a very practical need that made her become a professional writer: the need for money.

Louisa May Alcott was born on November 29, 1832, in Pennsylvania. Her father, Amos Bronson Alcott, was an educator whom many people considered a genius. But for many years he was unable to support his family, and Louisa's youth was one of scanty meals and hand-me-down clothes. Her dream was to make the family's fortune so that her mother could spend her days in comfort.

But how? She tried the usual careers open to women at that time. She sewed (by hand —sewing machines had been invented but were not yet common), she taught school, and she acted as a companion to an invalid lady. These jobs produced a living, but scarcely a fortune. Then, when she was 19, a story of hers was bought and published by a magazine, and she determined to try writing for a living.

It took her some time to decide what she should write. Her first book was published when she was 22. It was a collection of fairy

An illustration from *Little Women*. The experiences of the March family were drawn from Alcott's own life.

tales, *Flower Fables,* which she had written six years earlier. But her first real success was *Hospital Sketches*. It recounted her experiences as a Civil War nurse and was written under the pen name Tribulation Periwinkle. Alcott also wrote two novels, now forgotten, which got mixed reviews. For some time, most of her earnings came from magazine stories. These were romantic, often tragic tales of far-off places and strange happenings in the lives of artists and actresses. Some, of a type called sensation stories, dealt with murder and madness, sinister noblemen, and wicked guardians. They were so bloodcurdling that she wouldn't let her own name appear on them.

In 1867, Alcott became editor of *Merry's Museum,* a magazine for children, and a publisher asked her to write a book for girls. At first she refused—that wasn't what she was used to writing. Then she suddenly realized that she had just such a story right at hand— she and her sisters had lived it.

A WRITER AND HER IMAGE

Jo March of *Little Women* is, in many ways, a self-portrait of Louisa May Alcott. Jo's temper, her tomboyish ways, her impatience with fashionable follies—all these Louisa shared. But most important, Jo, like her creator, was a writer. And as these excerpts from *Little Women* show, her writing career mirrors Louisa's. Their methods of writing were the same:

Every few weeks [Jo] would shut herself up in her room, put on her scribbling suit, and "fall into a vortex," as she expressed it, writing away at her novel with all her heart and soul, for till that was finished she could find no peace. Her "scribbling suit" consisted of a black woolen pinafore on which she could wipe her pen at will, and a cap of the same material, adorned with a cheerful red bow, into which she bundled her hair when the decks were cleared for action. This cap was a beacon to the inquiring eyes of her family, who

during these periods kept their distance, merely popping in their heads semioccasionally, to ask, with interest, "Does genius burn, Jo?" They did not always venture even to ask this question, but took an observation of the cap and judged accordingly. If this expressive article of dress was drawn low upon the forehead, it was a sign that hard work was going on; in exciting moments it was pushed rakishly askew; and when despair seized the author it was plucked wholly off, and cast upon the floor. At such times the intruder silently withdrew; and not until the red bow was seen gaily erect upon the gifted brow did anyone dare address Jo.

She did not think herself a genius by any means; but when the writing fit came on, she gave herself up to it with entire abandon, and led a blissful life, unconscious of want, care or bad weather, while she sat safe and happy in an imaginary world, full of friends almost as real and dear to her as any in the flesh. Sleep forsook her eyes, meals stood untasted, day and night were all too short to enjoy the happiness which blessed her only at such times, and made these hours worth living, even if they bore no other fruit. The divine afflatus usually lasted a week or two, and then she emerged from her "vortex" hungry, sleepy, cross, or despondent.

Both Louisa and Jo earned money from "sensation stories" that they were more than half ashamed of:

Jo . . . was just beginning to give up all hope of ever seeing her manuscript again when a letter arrived which almost took her breath away; for on opening it, a check for a hundred dollars fell into her lap. For a minute she stared at it as if it had been a snake, then she read her letter and began to cry. If the amiable gentleman who wrote that kindly note could have known what intense happiness he was giving a fellow creature, I think he would devote his leisure hours, if he has any, to that amusement; for Jo valued the letter more than the money, because it was encouraging; and after years of effort it was *so* pleasant to find that she had learned to do something, though it was only to write a sensation story.

. . . .

Jo fell to work with a cheery spirit, bent on earning more of those delightful checks. She did earn several that year, and began to feel herself a power in the house; for by the magic of a pen, her "rubbish" turned into comforts for them all. "The Duke's Daughter" paid the butcher's bill, "A Phantom Hand" put down a new carpet, and the "Curse of the Coventrys" proved the blessing of the Marches in the way of groceries and gowns.

Thus the first part of *Little Women* was written. A far cry from her blood-and-thunder tales, it tells the story of four girls growing up in a small New England town in the mid-1800's. The characters were drawn from her family and from people she knew. Alcott based Jo March, the main character, on herself. The character of Laurie, the boy next door, was based on two old friends.

The first volume was a success, and she wrote the second part of *Little Women* soon after. Louisa May Alcott had finally found the type of writing that would bring her fame and fortune.

The Books. *Little Women* (1868–1869) quickly became one of the most widely read novels for young people, and it is still in demand. It is popular because it portrays young people with freshness, humor, and accuracy. Meg, Jo, Beth, and Amy March relive the joys and sorrows of Anna, Louisa, Elizabeth, and Abby May Alcott. Many of the incidents and situations in the book—the family theatricals, Meg's marriage, Beth's death, Jo's writing career, even the sensation stories—were taken from the Alcotts' lives. But the author, who never married, invented more freely toward the end, when she married Jo off to a German professor. The sequels, *Little Men* (1871) and *Jo's Boys* (1886), tell of the school that Jo and the professor founded and of the boys and girls who grew up there.

An Old-Fashioned Girl (1870) is about Polly Milton. Her rich, frivolous friends the Shaws consider her "old-fashioned" because she is hardworking, wholesome, and independent. But they come to value her goodness.

Eight Cousins (1875) and its sequel, *Rose in Bloom* (1876), tell of Rose Campbell, her friend and adoptive sister Phebe, and her seven boy cousins. Under the care of her Uncle Alec, orphaned Rose grows from a fretful and sickly child into a healthy, strong-minded woman.

In *Under the Lilacs* (1878), Ben, a circus boy, and his performing poodle, Sancho, find a home with a kind lady and her convalescent brother.

Jack and Jill (1880) is the story of poor Janey ("Jill") Pecq and well-off Jack Minot, good friends who are hurt in a sledding acci-

dent. The story is set in a village similar to Concord, Massachusetts, where Alcott spent much of her youth.

A. A. MILNE (1882–1956)

Alan Alexander Milne was born on January 18, 1882, in London. After graduating from Cambridge University, he set out to make a living as a writer. And he succeeded, writing plays and novels and essays.

In 1920, Milne and his wife had a son, Christopher Robin. Milne watched as his son played with stuffed toy animals and went off with his nanny to the zoo or to see the changing of the guard at Buckingham Palace. Remembering his own happy childhood, Milne began to write poems—poems about the games and pranks of childhood, about its toys and stories, about the animals children love and the countryside as they see it. These poems were collected and published

THE KING'S BREAKFAST
by A. A. Milne

The King asked
The Queen, and
The Queen asked
The Dairymaid:
"Could we have some butter for
The Royal slice of bread?"
The Queen asked
The Dairymaid,
The Dairymaid
Said, "Certainly,
I'll go and tell
The cow
Now
Before she goes to bed."

The Dairymaid
She curtsied,
And went and told
The Alderney:
"Don't forget the butter for
The Royal slice of bread."

The Alderney
Said sleepily:

"You'd better tell
His Majesty
That many people nowadays
Like marmalade
Instead."

The Dairymaid
Said, "Fancy!"
And went to
Her Majesty.
She curtsied to the Queen, and
She turned a little red:
"Excuse me,
Your Majesty,
For taking of
The liberty,
But marmalade is tasty, if
It's very
Thickly
Spread."

The Queen said
"Oh!"
And went to
His Majesty:
"Talking of the butter for
The Royal slice of bread,
Many people
Think that

Christopher Robin, Tigger, Pooh, Eeyore, and Piglet.

in *When We Were Very Young* and *Now We Are Six,* with the illustrations by Ernest H. Shepard.

Meanwhile, in 1925, the Milnes had bought a house in the country, Crotchford Farm, where they went during the summer and on holidays. It was a new world for Christopher Robin. There was a stream, woods to ramble through, and an ancient walnut tree with a hollow just big enough for him and his toy bear. There were live animals, too—owls in the woods, rabbits on the hillside, cats in the yard, and a mouse that wandered into his room.

Again Milne watched his son at play. And he began to write stories of the doings of Christopher Robin and his stuffed toy animals—and a few wild animals as well. He read the stories aloud in the evenings, and his wife encouraged him to publish them. Shepard drew the pictures, and *Winnie-the-Pooh* and *The House at Pooh Corner* soon appeared.

The Books. *When We Were Very Young* (1924) and *Now We Are Six* (1927) are books of poems. Some are about Christopher Robin, some about things Milne did as a

Marmalade
Is nicer.
Would you like to try a little
Marmalade
Instead?"

The King said,
"Bother!"
And then he said,
"Oh, dear me!"
The King sobbed, "Oh, deary me!"
And went back to bed.
"Nobody,"
He whimpered,
"Could call me
A fussy man;
I *only* want
A little bit
Of butter for
My bread!"

The Queen said,
"There, there!"
And went to

The Dairymaid.
The Dairymaid
Said, "There, there!"
And went to the shed.
The cow said,
"There, there!
I didn't really

Mean it;
Here's milk for his porringer
And butter for his bread."

The Queen took
The butter
And brought it to
His Majesty;
The King said,
"Butter, eh?"
And bounced out of bed.
"Nobody," he said,
As he kissed her
Tenderly,
"Nobody," he said,
As he slid down
The banisters,
"Nobody,
My darling,
Could call me
A fussy man—
BUT

I do like a little bit of butter to my bread!"

child, and some about things any child might do. A few of the poems ("Daffodowndilly," "The Mirror," and "The Invaders") are nature poems.

When children play with dolls or stuffed animals, they often pretend that the toys are characters, with lives of their own. This was how Christopher Robin played with his stuffed animals—the bear, Winnie-the-Pooh; Piglet; Eeyore, the donkey; Kanga and Roo; and the bouncing Tigger. And this is how Milne pictures them in *Winnie-the-Pooh* (1926) and *The House at Pooh Corner* (1928).

Each animal has a house in the Hundred Acre Wood—as do Owl, Rabbit, and Rabbit's many friends and relations, all of whom Milne made up. They visit each other and have tea and birthday parties. They go hunting for strange beasts—Woozles and Heffalumps. They go on "expotitions" (expeditions) to find the North Pole or one of Rabbit's friends. And they cope with the weather —a flood that strands Piglet; a snowstorm that prompts them to build Eeyore a house; a mist in which Rabbit, Pooh, and Piglet get lost; and a wind that blows down Owl's house.

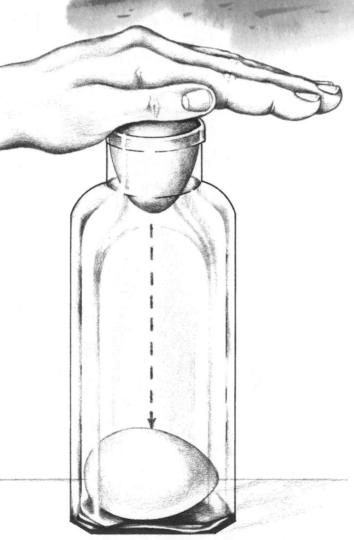

After a 24-hour soak in vinegar, the shell of a hard-boiled egg becomes so soft and flexible you can squeeze the egg into a bottle.

EGG-SPERIMENTS

You don't need lots of fancy equipment to learn some interesting facts about eggs. Here are four activities. Use them to impress your family and friends. Be an egg-sperimenter!

THE RUBBER EGG

The shell of an egg is hard because it contains a lot of calcium. You can get rid of the calcium and make a "rubber" egg.

Take a raw egg and place it in a glass. Pour vinegar into the glass until it completely covers the egg. Let the egg stand in the vinegar for 24 hours. Vinegar is an acid, and it will dissolve the calcium compound in the eggshell. Only a thin, rubbery skin will be left around the raw inside.

You can watch the vinegar at work. About an hour after you start this egg-speriment, you will see bubbles on the surface of the eggshell. The bubbles are a gas that forms when the vinegar reacts with the calcium compound.

After 24 hours, remove the egg from the glass. Compare it with a regular raw egg. Do they look the same? Do they feel the same?

You can gently squeeze your rubber egg. Don't squeeze too hard, though, or you will break the egg.

The rubber egg can only be kept for about a day. After that, it will begin to get soggy.

Here is an interesting variation on this egg-speriment: Make a rubber bone. Put a chicken wishbone or leg bone in a glass of vinegar. It takes about three days for the vinegar to dissolve the calcium in a wishbone, and about a week for the leg bone to soften.

BOTTLE AN EGG

This egg-speriment is very similar to the rubber egg egg-speriment. Now, however, start with a hard-boiled egg. You'll also need a bottle with a neck that is a little smaller than the diameter of the egg.

Place the hard-boiled egg in vinegar for 24 hours, until the calcium compound has been dissolved and the shell is soft and flexible. Then take the egg and squeeze it into the bottle. You can actually push the egg through the neck of the bottle without breaking the egg. When the egg falls into the wider part of the bottle, it will regain its shape.

RAW? OR HARD-BOILED?

You take an egg out of the refrigerator to make a chopped egg sandwich. But you're not sure if the egg is raw or hard-boiled. To find out, you can break the egg. Here is a better way to decide:

Spin the egg on a plate or on the top of the kitchen table. Lightly touch the top of the spinning egg with your finger to slow down the egg. Quickly lift your finger from the egg.

If the egg is hard-boiled, it will stop spinning. But if the egg is raw, it will continue to spin a little longer.

The hard-boiled egg is solid all the way through. Therefore it acts as one unit. When you touch and stop the shell, the inside of the egg stops, too. A raw egg doesn't act as one unit. The shell is solid but the raw inside is liquid. When you stop the shell, the liquid inside is not stopped. It will keep the egg spinning after you have taken your finger off the shell.

THE FLOATER

What happens when you put a fresh raw egg in a glass of water? The egg is denser (heavier) than water, so it sinks to the bottom. But with a little trickery you can make the egg float in the middle of the glass.

If you put a fresh raw egg in a glass of water, it will sink to the bottom. But with a little salt and skill, you can make the egg float in the middle of the glass.

Put three tablespoons of salt in the glass. Half-fill the glass with water. Stir the water until all the salt has dissolved.

Gently set the raw egg on the water. The egg will float on the surface because it isn't as dense as the salt water.

With a funnel, slowly pour fresh water on top of the egg. This must be done very carefully—you don't want the fresh water and salt water to mix. Keep adding fresh water until the glass is full.

Where is the egg? Right in the middle of the glass. The egg will continue to float on the denser salt water but remain at the bottom of the fresh water. Of course, the dividing line between the two types of water is invisible, so friends will believe that you are an egg-spert magician.

There is another way to make an egg float in a glass of water. The density of an egg changes as the egg ages. Old eggs are not as dense as fresh eggs because they have begun to dry out. As you have seen, fresh eggs sink to the bottom of a glass of water. But stale eggs will float partly up the glass. The staler the egg, the higher it will float. This is also a way to test an egg's freshness without breaking the shell.

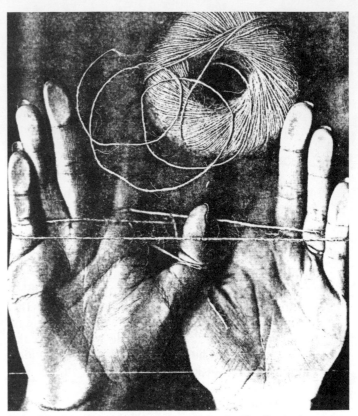

Twine Time, by Connie Hedgepath, 17, Louisville, Kentucky

YOUNG PHOTOGRAPHERS

What's behind the green door? What would the world be like if you were only a few inches tall? Young people are curious about the world. They often see common things—a pair of shoes or a ball of string—in a new way. A camera lets them capture what they see and share their insights with us.

The photographs on these and the following pages were among the winners in the 1982 Scholastic/Kodak Photo Awards program. The program offers scholarships and other awards to talented young photographers. It is open to junior and senior high school students in the United States and Canada.

What do young people hope to accomplish through photography? The winner of the 1982 contest described his goals this way: "I want to reach people, to make them understand what I see, and ultimately, change society a fraction for the better."

Green Door, by Barbara Green, 17, Reseda, California

Untitled,
by David Beck, 16,
East Canton, Ohio

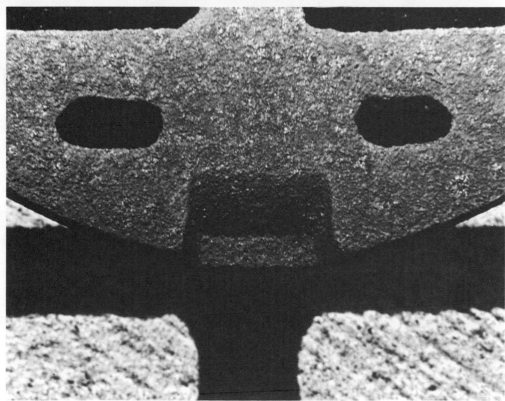

The Face,
by Mike Best, 17,
Raleigh, North Carolina

Shells, by Joe Funkhouse, 17, Largo, Florida

Giants, by David Marteeny, 17, Daytona Beach, Florida

Detail in Green,
by Amy Zabinski, 15,
Buffalo, New York

Silent Rain,
by Nancy Baker, 17,
Williamson, New York

FANTASY FLOWERS

You can create your own world of fantasy flowers. These colorful flowers are paper cutouts—pieces of colored paper cut out and glued one on top of another. Each piece is smaller than the piece beneath it. Notice, too, that the flowers are symmetrical—the left side of each flower is a mirror image of the right side.

A POLISH TRADITION

This craft originated long ago in Poland, where it is called *wycinanki*. Poles who lived on farms found that cutting out flowers, roosters, and other designs was a pleasant way to spend a long winter evening. It was also an inexpensive way to create decorations for a home.

Each spring, Polish peasants would wash and paint the walls of their homes. Then they would put up the paper cutouts they had made during the winter. Old, dusty cutouts from the previous year would be taken

down. Sometimes the previous year's cutouts would be placed in barns, where they could be enjoyed as the peasants did their chores.

At first, each family made its own cutouts. But some people were more talented than others, and they began selling their cutouts to friends and neighbors. People who lived in cities saw some cutouts and liked them. They started to collect this art, frame it, and hang it in their apartments. Today, people all over the world recognize Polish paper cutouts as an important folk art.

HOW TO MAKE PAPER CUTOUTS

To make your own fantasy flowers, you will need paper in various colors (construction paper can be used), scissors, and white glue. Set aside several sheets of paper for the background.

Begin by making the largest, or bottom, piece of a flower. Fold the paper in half, then cut out the design. You can do this freehand —without a pattern—or you can first draw a pattern on the paper.

Now cut out the second largest piece, using a different color. Again, fold the paper in half. If you wish, you can trace the outline of the largest piece onto this paper. This will make it easier for you to cut a design that is smaller than the first piece and that will look well on top of it. A flower can have as many layers as you wish. Most Polish cutouts have three to five layers.

To cut the symmetrical side flowers, use two pieces of paper. Fold each in half. Place one folded piece inside the other and cut a design from both pieces at the same time. Cut the stem and leaves in one piece, using a sheet of green paper folded in half.

To assemble your design, first glue the stem and leaves onto the background paper. This piece should be centered on the paper. Next, attach the largest piece of each flower. Build up the flower layer by layer. Be careful to always center each piece on the underlying layer. The crease marks that formed when you folded the paper are a useful guide for centering.

ANIMALS ON VACATION

All the animals decided to take a vacation. They wanted to travel and see new places. The lamb went to LAMBach, Austria. The llama went to PaLLAMAna, Australia. And the ox went to KnOXville, Tennessee. Can you figure out where the following animals went? (You may want to use maps to help you.)

The hen went to Greece's capital.	_ _ HEN _
The bat flew to a city in Morocco.	_ _ BAT
The mite hiked through a national park in California.	_ _ _ _ MITE
The asp slithered north from Maine into Quebec.	_ ASP _ _ _ _ _ _ _ _ _
The dove flew along England's white cliffs.	DOVE _
The ape swung through this city in South Africa.	_ APE _ _ _ _
The ram visited the capital of California.	_ _ _ RAM _ _ _ _
The rat relaxed in a spa in New York.	_ _ RAT _ _ _ _ _ _ _ _ _ _
The horse galloped to the Yukon Territory . . . or did it go to South Dakota?	_ _ _ _ _ HORSE
The cow grazed its way to the capital of the Soviet Union.	_ _ _ COW
The otter swam to one of the biggest cities in the Netherlands.	_ OTTER _ _ _
The cat went to the east coast of Mexico.	_ _ CAT _ _
The ant crawled to a city in Texas.	_ _ _ ANT _ _ _ _
The hare hopped through the capital of Rumania.	_ _ _ HARE _ _

ANSWERS: Athens, Rabat, Yosemite, Gaspé Peninsula, Dover, Cape Town, Sacramento, Saratoga Springs, Whitehorse, Moscow, Rotterdam, Yucatan, San Antonio, Bucharest.

A JOURNEY
TO IMAGINARY PLACES

Have you ever been to a land where the farmers grow balloons? Not ordinary balloons—watermelon balloons, rye bread balloons, potato balloons, peach balloons, even sausage and pork chop balloons. In late summer, you can watch people get up on stilts to harvest the season's crops. Some use long stilts, others short ones. Baby pickers use baby stilts to pick baby balloons. Sometimes people fall off the stilts. But by holding onto several balloons, they stay aloft until they can get their feet onto the stilts again.

You could visit such a place—in your imagination. The Country of the Balloon Pickers is an imaginary land created by Carl Sandburg and described in his book *Rootabaga Stories*. There are many other special worlds in stories, poems, songs, and movies. Some are beautiful. Some are ugly or scary. And some are funny. Let's travel to a few of these imaginary places and see what they are like.

Next to the Country of the Balloon Pickers is Rootabaga Country, where rootabagas are a main crop and villages have such quaint names as Liver-and-Onions and Cream Puffs. A common garden flower is the necktie poppy. These poppies come in many different colors and patterns. One has "a picture like whiteface pony spots on a green frog swimming in the moonshine." Men pick necktie poppies to wear to work or when they go downtown to the post office.

The animals in Rootabaga Country are curious creatures. All the pigs wear bibs—striped pigs wear striped bibs, polka-dot pigs wear polka-dot bibs, and checkered pigs wear checkered bibs. Black cats wear orange and gold stockings. Squirrels carry ladders. Fish jump out of the rivers to talk to frying pans. And every night the frogs gamble, using gold dice.

IMAGINARY CAVES

In *The Patchwork Girl of Oz*, L. Frank Baum takes us to a magnificent marble cave lit by soft light from some unknown source. Two nations live in the cave: the Horners and the Hoppers. A high fence separates the two groups.

The Horners are short people, with heads and bodies like round balls. A typical Horner has pointed ears and a sharp, white horn in the center of the forehead. But the most striking feature is the hair. Around the face,

the hair is red. Above the red hair is a circle of yellow hair, and above that is a topknot of green hair. The Horners are ruled by a chief named Jak, who wears a star on top of his horn.

The Hoppers get their name from the fact that they have only one leg, and so they move from place to place by hopping. Relations between the Horners and the Hoppers are not always friendly.

Another underground country is described by Luc Alberny in *The Blue Mammoth*. Called Grande Euscarie, the country is located beneath the Basque region of France. It is inhabited by huge mammoths, who took refuge in the caves during the Ice Age, and by centaurs, who ruled the land before the arrival of the mammoths. The ruler today is the Blue Mammoth, who is known as King of the World.

Tourists will find Grande Euscarie an interesting place. It has a tropical climate and there is no night. The best souvenirs are the beautiful carpets made by the mammoths.

Many thousands of years ago the mammoths taught their language to the people who lived above the ground in the region. Today this is the Basque language. So if you visit the caves, make sure you take along a Basque dictionary.

In J. R. R. Tolkien's trilogy, *The Lord of the Rings,* there is a system of caves called Aglarond, or the Glittering Caves. The walls of the caves sparkle with gems, crystals, and veins of precious ores. There are beautifully colored pillars that are "fluted and twisted into dreamlike forms." Quiet lakes mirror the walls, columns, and glistening roof.

The caves lie beneath the mountains around Helm's Deep, a deep gorge in the kingdom of Rohan. For a long time, the caves were used mainly as a place to store materials. But during a great war, Gimli the dwarf, one of the defenders of Helm's Deep, visited the caves and saw their beauty and their immense size. "There is chamber after chamber," he said; "hall opening out of hall, dome after dome, stair beyond stair; and still the winding paths lead on into the mountains' heart.

"Happy was the chance that drove me there!" continued Gimli. "It makes me weep to leave them." When the war ended, Gimli

and some other dwarfs moved into the Glittering Caves and were very happy there (*above*).

IMAGINARY CITIES

The French composer Hector Berlioz created a city called Euphonia, which he placed in the Harz Mountains of Germany. The only activities of the Euphonians are musical ones. Some of the people sing or play musical instruments. Some compose music. Some teach music. Some do research on the physics of musical sounds.

A tall tower rises above the other buildings in Euphonia. At the top of the tower is a 500-year-old organ. Each morning, the organ sounds to announce the start of work. It sounds again when the working day is over. By means of a special musical code understood only by Euphonians, the organ also gives people instructions, presents general information, and otherwise serves as a communications center.

It may be very difficult for you to visit Euphonia. In order to be allowed to enter the city, a person must have a superb voice, be able to play almost every musical instrument, and pass a personality test.

A much larger and more famous city is the Emerald City, the capital of L. Frank Baum's marvelous land of Oz (*below*). Built by the Wizard of Oz, this city is best known for the sparkling emeralds that decorate almost every structure. The houses, streets, and sidewalks are made of marble studded with emeralds. And in the glorious Royal Palace, there seem to be jewels everywhere. The most beautiful room in the palace is the high-domed, circular throne room, which is completely encrusted with large emeralds. The baths in the palace are made of marble and are big enough to swim in, and all the beds are made of gold.

The Emerald City is surrounded by a high, thick wall. There is only one entrance into the city, through a gate covered with emeralds. This entrance is guarded by a man with long green whiskers. But the city's main protection against unfriendly outsiders is the love magnet that hangs over the entranceway and makes everyone who enters Emerald City a loving—and lovable—person.

A very different city is Dictionopolis, created by Norton Juster in *The Phantom Tollbooth.* Dictionopolis is the source of all the words in the world. The words are grown in orchards. Once a week, people gather in the marketplace to buy words and to sell those words they haven't used. People who want to make up their own words can buy individual letters. But you should find out how the letters taste before you buy any. A is very tasty. C is crunchy. I is cool and refreshing. X tastes stale and Z tastes like sawdust. These different tastes help explain why letters such as A, C, and I often appear in words while letters such as X and Z are seldom used.

The rival of Dictionopolis is Digitopolis. This city, ruled by the Mathemagician, is the source of all numbers. The numbers are taken from the numbers mine, polished, and shipped to all parts of the world. Some numbers are broken during mining or polishing; these are used as fractions.

If you visit Digitopolis, take care not to eat the subtraction stew. The more you eat, the hungrier you'll become!

IMAGINARY FORESTS

In *Figures of Earth* and *The High Place,* James Branch Cabell describes Acaire, a huge forest inhabited by monsters such as the eale, which has movable horns, and the tarandus, which is always the color of its surroundings. On a mountain in Acaire stands the castle of King Helmas. Helmas has a daughter named Melusine. One day, Helmas and Melusine had a fight. Melusine put her father, mother, and their followers into a sleep from which they still have not awakened. This was a terrible thing to do, and Melusine was punished for her behavior. Every Sunday her legs turn into the tail of a fish—and they remain like that until Monday.

In *Tarzan and the Ant Men,* Edgar Rice Burroughs tells about the people who live in the Great Thorn Forest. The Ant Men are only a few inches high. They ride tiny antelopes and live in domed houses sometimes called anthills by outsiders. The only other people in the forest are the Alali. Gigantic

women rule the Alali village. Boys are treated very poorly there. They are kept in pens until they are about 15 years old. Then they are sent out into the forest. Some are later captured and kept as slaves.

If you want to visit an imaginary forest, perhaps the best place to go is the Forest of Sight, which lies north of Dictionopolis. The Bing family lives there—and what an unusual family it is! Each member sees things in a different way. One sees through things, another sees beyond things, still another sees under things, and still another sees after things. And one sees the other side of the question.

The Bings are born quite truly with "their feet off the ground"—their heads are at the height they will be when they become adults. And instead of growing upward, like most people, the Bings grow downward. By the time they reach adulthood, their feet touch the ground.

Of course, you don't have to visit someone else's imaginary cave, city, or forest. You can create your own imaginary places, filled with your own imaginary people.

THUMPER'S LUCKY STREAK

Bambi and Thumper nosed through the sweet clover in the patch on the edge of the forest. Thumper buried his face deep in the fragrant grass for another bite. He stopped short. Standing up out of the small patch was a four-leaf clover.

"What a great good luck charm!" said Thumper as he snatched the clover up in his paw. "Now I'm sure to win the Forest Olympics race."

"You'll win anyway," said Bambi. "You've been practicing all spring. You must be the fastest runner in the forest by now."

All the same, Thumper wove the clover into a grass chain so he could wear it around his neck. He felt very lucky now.

In the days before the race, Thumper doubled his training effort. He doubled the number of stretching exercises to limber and tone his muscles. He trotted double the distance to build up his endurance. He doubled his practice laps around the race track.

And he also doubled his reasons for believing in his lucky four-leaf clover.

First, Thumper's biggest competitor, a rabbit named Streak, pulled a muscle and had to drop out of the race.

This moved Thumper's starting position from number eight to number seven. As he pointed out to Bambi, "Seven has always been my lucky number. Now I have twice the luck, and I don't have to worry about Streak.''

"It wasn't very lucky for Streak,'' Bambi replied. "I don't think you should count someone's bad luck as your good fortune.''

Thumper didn't argue, but he patted his good luck charm. Bambi knew he would go on believing in luck instead of in himself.

The day before the race, Bambi watched Thumper run his last practice lap. The little rabbit flew around the track, his feet barely touching the ground.

"That was the fastest yet,'' called Bambi, trotting over to his friend.

"Thanks to my lucky clover,'' panted Thumper. "I've been getting faster every day.''

That night all the forest animals settled down early. Everyone wanted to be rested for the Forest Olympics. There would be hopping competitions for frogs and toads, antler sparring for the deer, an acorn toss for the squirrels and chipmunks, and digging competitions for the rabbits, moles, and gophers. But everyone looked forward most to the day's final event—the big race. It was

the most exciting. And since it was open to all animals, everyone knew someone who was running.

When the morning light filtered through the forest, Bambi went to get his friend Thumper, and found him still asleep.

His nose twitched and his paws moved back and forth. His front paw clutched the four-leaf clover he wore around his neck. Thumper was dreaming about the race.

Bambi nosed him gently. "It's almost time for the first event,'' he whispered.

Thumper's eyes shot open. "Who won?'' he asked.

"You will,'' said Bambi.

When Bambi and Thumper arrived at the staging area, the hopping competition was just getting under way.

Frogs and toads from every part of the forest were lined up in front of a large stag who was calling out the rules.

"You will hop straight up on the count of three,'' he shouted as he paced back and forth in front of the competitors. "The opossums are stationed in the trees to judge the jumps from the air. The highest jump wins.''

The stag counted to three. Suddenly it

looked like it was raining frogs and toads—all sizes, shapes, and colors. When they had all landed, the winner was named, and a thin, green frog with brown spots hopped up to receive his prize.

Antler sparring was the next event. One by one, the stags bowed their heads and locked antlers in a test of strength, until the strongest stag won.

Event by event, the Forest Olympics continued. A chipmunk that Thumper knew won the acorn toss. A mole waddled up to take the prize in the digging competition.

Thumper was getting impatient, so he did some stretching exercises. Finally Owl stepped up to start the big race. He waved his large gray wings over his head. "Time for the race," he hooted. "All runners line up."

Thumper started to hop toward the starting line. Suddenly he stopped short. "My lucky charm," he gasped, feeling for the four-leaf clover that had been hanging around his neck. "It's gone!" He turned to Bambi with large, frightened eyes.

"Oh, Bambi! Help me find it!" Thumper raced in wild circles, frantically searching for the lost clover.

Owl was calling the runners to hurry into position.

"Forget the clover," said Bambi. "You don't have time to find it. And you don't need it anyway."

"But I *do* need it," wailed Thumper. "I can't win the race without my charm!"

Bambi saw that Thumper wouldn't believe him. He turned and disappeared into a thicket. Minutes later he returned with a shining silver feather.

"I wouldn't give this to anyone else," he said, solemnly passing the feather to Thumper. "This is from the majestic eagle. It's the most powerful good luck charm I know, but it works only once. Now go out there and *win!*"

Thumper raced off to the starting line, the silver feather clutched tightly in his teeth. Just as he skidded to a stop at the starting line, Owl began to screech: "Ready! Set! Goowwhhoo!"

A cloud of dust flew up as rabbits, deer, squirrels, foxes, and skunks stormed down the track. There was so much dust that Bambi couldn't see who was in front. Then, as the cloud raced past, he saw a red fox take the lead. The dust cloud was approaching the finish line. Thumper nosed out in front, still holding the feather. Then the fox put on a burst of speed and moved up again. Then it was Thumper . . . then the fox . . . then Thumper, as he zoomed across the finish line first!

"And the winner," Owl hooted loudly, "is Thumper!"

The crowd cheered, and all the rabbits thumped the ground with their hind feet.

Thumper happily hopped over to Owl to take his prize.

Owl eyed Thumper closely. "Where did you get that feather?" he asked.

Thumper dropped it. "Bambi gave it to me. It's a lucky feather from the majestic eagle. I couldn't have won without it."

"Oh, paws and claws!" laughed Owl. "That's one of my very own tail feathers. Bambi asked me for it right before the race."

Thumper was confused.

"Listen, Thumper," Owl continued, "owl feathers would make you smart, not lucky. And if you were smart, you'd know that luck doesn't win a race. Hard work, ability, and self-confidence do. Lucky majestic eagle feather, indeed!"

Thumper took his prize and hopped off to find Bambi. He had some apologizing to do.

On their way home from the Forest Olympics, Bambi and Thumper stopped at their favorite clover patch. Thumper buried his nose in the sweet grass and thought how wonderful it tasted. Suddenly he saw another four-leaf clover. This time Thumper gobbled it right down.

CRAZY ABOUT CATS

For centuries, cats have been praised in stories, songs, and poems. They have been a favorite subject for painters and sculptors. And they have been loved by their owners for their elegance, their intelligence, their independence, their tidy habits, and their amusing ways.

But suddenly cats have become more than lovable, cuddly creatures. They have become superstars. People have simply gone crazy over cats. Everywhere you look, you'll see them. Books and calendars featuring felines have become best-sellers. So have mugs, glasses, T-shirts, towels, and other items decorated with cats.

Cats have become so popular that some people have even been imitating them. In late 1982, a rock musical titled *Cats* stalked onto Broadway. The hit show was based on T. S. Eliot's 1939 book of whimsical poems, *Old Possum's Book of Practical Cats*. Everyone in the show's cast acted like a cat. The performers walked and leaped like cats.

They sat in strange catlike positions. They constantly washed themselves, licking hands held like paws.

SUPERCATS

One of the people most responsible for the recent cat craze is artist Bernard Kliban. In 1975, he published a book called *Cat,* which has taken the world by storm. Kliban's cats are gray striped tabbies. They are fairly ordinary looking felines—except that they can often be seen wearing sneakers or roller skates, and sometimes they don sweaters, party hats, or flippers and a snorkel. Kliban's tabbies reflect his definition of a cat—something that is "frequently mistaken for a meatloaf."

Kliban's cats are nameless. But other supercats have names that are known everywhere. Heathcliff is a pudgy orange tomcat created by George Gately. Heathcliff is a smart, tough fellow who is as much at home in an alley as he is in an ice-cream parlor (where he likes to order raw fish). In addition to appearing in newspaper cartoons, Heathcliff starred in two animated TV specials.

Another supercat who starred in an animated TV special is Garfield. Garfield is a bossy, overweight, out-of-shape alley cat created by Jim Davis. "I never met a lasagna I didn't like," says Garfield. It's no wonder he gets fatter and fatter! But even Garfield admits it's time to diet when he can no longer drag his big belly to the refrigerator.

Garfield seems ready to eat everything and anything. Morris is different. He is what is known as a finicky eater. This orange cat will only eat one brand of cat food, which he advertises on television and in magazines and newspapers. A few years ago, his popularity led to his receiving a Patsy Award (the Academy Award of the animal world) for "outstanding performance in a TV commercial."

Walt Disney's supercat is Big, Bad Pete—Mickey Mouse's first and worst enemy. Pete is a large, tough black and white cat who is always trying to pull off the perfect crime. In late 1983, Pete will return to the movie

In the rock musical *Cats,* all the performers slinked, hissed, and stalked across the stage.

THE NAMING OF CATS

The Naming of Cats is a difficult matter,
    It isn't just one of your holiday games;
You may think at first I'm as mad as a hatter
    When I tell you a cat must have THREE
    DIFFERENT NAMES.
First of all, there's the name that the family use
    daily,
    Such as Peter, Augustus, Alonzo or James,
Such as Victor or Jonathan, George or Bill Bailey—
    All of them sensible everyday names.
There are fancier names if you think they sound
    sweeter,
    Some for the gentlemen, some for the dames:
Such as Plato, Admetus, Electra, Demeter—
    But all of them sensible everyday names.
But I tell you, a cat needs a name that's particular,
    A name that's peculiar, and more dignified,
Else how can he keep up his tail perpendicular,
    Or spread out his whiskers, or cherish his
    pride?
Of names of this kind, I can give you a quorum,
    Such as Munkustrap, Quaxo or Coricopat,
Such as Bombalurina, or else Jellylorum—
    Names that never belong to more than one cat.
But above and beyond there's still one name left
    over,
    And that is the name that you will never guess;
The name that no human research can discover—
    BUT THE CAT HIMSELF KNOWS, and will
    never confess.
When you notice a cat in profound meditation,
    The reason, I tell you, is always the same:
His mind is engaged in a rapt contemplation
    Of the thought, of the thought, of the thought
    of his name:
    His ineffable effable
    Effanineffable
Deep and inscrutable singular Name.

T. S. ELIOT (1888–1965)
Old Possum's Book of Practical Cats

screen as the Ghost of Christmas Future in *Mickey's Christmas Carol.*

SUPERBREEDS

Cats have also been clawing their way up to the top of the pet popularity polls. More people than ever before own one of these purr-fect pets.

There are many different kinds, or breeds, of cats. The most common and best known is the domestic shorthair. You have probably also heard of Siamese, Abyssinian, Persian, and Burmese cats. But have you ever heard of . . .

The Rex. The Rex cat has big ears that often seem too large for its head. But the Rex is primarily known for its coat, which is so short and curly that the cat looks like it's had a permanent wave. Surprisingly, the dense hair is extremely soft and silky. Rex cats are a new breed. The first known Rex was born on a farm in England in 1950. Its parents were domestic shorthairs. A Rex may be any of the many colors found among domestic shorthairs, including tabby and calico mixtures. Rex cats are very affectionate. And, unlike most other cats, a Rex may wag its tail when it is happy. Because of this and because of their curly coats, Rex cats are sometimes called "poodle cats."

The Korat. This short-haired, silver-blue cat originated in Thailand long, long ago. It has a heart-shaped head with large, luminous green eyes. The Korat is known for its sweet and loving nature and fine disposition. The people of Thailand think of it as a "good luck" cat.

The Rex

The Japanese Bobtail. This slender, medium-sized cat has a short, bunnylike tail that resembles a pom-pom. It has a triangular head, large ears, and slanted eyes. It may be pure white, black, or red, or a combination of these colors. In Japan, many people believe the Bobtail brings good luck. And Japanese artists often paint this cat with one paw raised in greeting.

The Chocolate-Mitted Ragdoll. In color, this cat looks very much like a long-haired Siamese. It's a gentle animal with—you guessed it—chocolate-colored paws. The Ragdoll is not considered a "true" breed.

The Somali. This cat is a long-haired version of the Abyssinian. It has an orange-brown or reddish coat, and each hair is individually ticked with black or brown. The large, almond-shaped eyes are gold or green. The spirited Somali has a habit of pacing back and forth, which gives it the appearance of a small mountain lion. But it is much better behaved and easier to handle!

The Maine Coon. In the 1850's, travelers brought long-haired cats from foreign lands to the state of Maine. The foreign cats mated with the local short-haired cats. The result was a new breed of cat that resembled a raccoon. Some people mistakenly thought the long-haired cats were the result of matings between cats and raccoons, hence the name Maine Coon. Maine Coons are large and muscular with thick, shaggy coats and long bushy tails. Like domestic shorthairs, Maine Coon cats may be any of many colors. They are gentle but rugged cats that can endure harsh climates.

The Maine Coon

The Somali
The Chocolate-Mitted Ragdoll

The Korat

THE PAPER BAG PLAYERS

"I won't take a bath!" the young boy insists. And so the battle begins. But the young boy is not arguing with his mother and father, or any other adult. Instead, he is arguing with a bathtub and a bar of soap! And they wheedle, coax, and cajole the boy to get himself clean.

This fantastic scene is not part of a cartoon. It is part of a skit acted by a unique theater group called the Paper Bag Players. An adult actor plays the role of the young boy, and two other performers play his adversaries. Their costumes are simply large cardboard props resembling a boy, a bathtub, and a bar of soap. The audience, consisting mostly of young children, laughs delightedly at the comic exchange. The idea of a talking bathtub is funny enough, but the audience laughs also because the scene is so familiar. Is there any youngster who has never balked at taking a bath?

STARTED ON A SHOESTRING

The Paper Bag Players were formed in 1958. Since then, the "Bags" have become one of the best, and most original, children's theater groups in the world. Perhaps because they were started on a shoestring, the Bags learned to use the simplest everyday objects as costumes and props—cardboard boxes, string, newspapers, brooms, aluminum foil, umbrellas, and of course, paper bags. And therein lies part of their charm. The audience feels comfortably close to these familiar objects, which have been magically transformed into cities, castles, chickens, and flowers.

Judith Martin has been with the Bags since she helped found the group, and she serves as performer, director, writer, and designer. She and other Bags performers have been known to search rubbish heaps for suitable trash to serve as scenery and props. And just

From the skit "Shoes": If two people feel happy and want to dance, big feet don't get in the way.

as she looks for her equipment in the back lots of everyday life, she also searches for ideas for skits in the everyday world: baths, working mothers, ice cream cones, crowded tenements, leaky faucets. An audience, she says, can relate to these contemporary things far better than to the fairy tales of more traditional children's theater.

The Bags' featured actor is Irving Burton, who has been described as a "performing genius." His characterizations combine acting, singing, and a broad range of movement including mime and dance. Eccentric and full of joyous humor, he is believable even when playing a bathtub, an ice cream cone, or somebody's mom.

There are other talented performers, plus the extra dimension of Donald Ashwander's music. With his electric harpsichord and various small instruments, Ashwander singlehandedly supplies the Bags' lively musical accompaniment—all his own compositions.

The audience's reaction is exuberant and spontaneous, and they sometimes take part in the action. In the middle of a skit, Burton, alone on stage, may leave a message for Martin with the audience. Burton departs, Martin comes on stage, and the spectators become active participants as they scream out Burton's message.

Most of the Bags' skits are only a few minutes long, but they are filled with witty comedy. A giant pair of lips jumps off a lipstick ad on a billboard and chases an ice cream cone; a carton of milk comes out of a cardboard cow; a street cleaner falls in love with his sweepings and dances with the trash.

The longer plays are just as fanciful. In "Everybody, Everybody," the Bags show how people from different cultures do things differently—but each culture thinks its own way is the right way. "Dandelion," which is about 70 minutes long, is very ambitious; it tells the history of life on Earth. One performer, in a large brown paper bag, plays Earth itself. His antics and gyrations, in the bag, demonstrate how the young Earth cooled down, grew mountains, and produced life. We meet the dinosaur, the fish, and the ape, and we find out how a flower reproduces. By the time "Dandelion" is over, the audience has learned a lot about evolution, laughing all the way.

In their 25 years of existence, the Paper Bag Players have performed in many places around the world. Their humor and ideas are so clear that language barriers seem to present little problem. The Bags' talents have not gone unnoticed. They were the first children's theater group to win an Obie (Off-Broadway Award) and the first to gain support from the National Endowment for the Arts. It seems that a lot of people enjoy an argument between a boy and a bar of soap!

By the way, if you are wondering about the ending of the skit called "I Won't Take a Bath," one more character makes an appearance—a gigantic cardboard mother. And the argument is over! SPLASH!

STICK 'EM UPS

The door of your refrigerator has become a bulletin board. Your family is putting all sorts of items on it—memos, cartoons, recipes, drawings. They are using magnets to attach these items to the refrigerator. But they aren't using ordinary magnets; they are using decorated magnets that you have made.

To make these impressive magnets, you will need decorations; bases made of wood or cardboard; glue; a sealer; and a roll of special tape that is magnetized on one side.

Start by choosing or making the decorations. Here are some possibilities: seashells, jewelry and buttons, dried beans and peas, various kinds of pasta, coins and stamps, decals and stickers, and pictures from magazines, newspapers, and comic books.

Now decide what type of base would look best with each decoration. If the decoration is round, you may want a round base. If it is square, a square base may be best.

If you are making wooden bases, use wood that is no more than ¾ inch (2 centimeters) thick. A good size for a square base would be 2 inches by 2 inches (5 centimeters by 5 centimeters). Have one of your parents help you saw the wood and sand the rough edges.

You may want to stain or paint the base before you attach the decoration. For in-

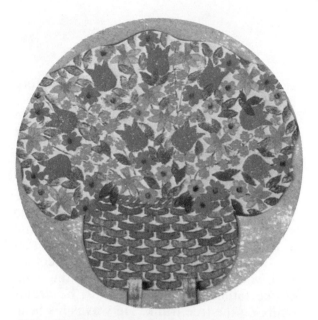

stance, a picture of a pink pig would be nice on a bright green background. A pinwheel design made from elbow macaroni would look striking on a red background. Or you can paint the background to match the colors of your kitchen.

Attach the decorations with glue. To keep them from coming loose and to prevent "edible" decorations from attracting insects, you should seal the surface. Try a water-based sealer or an acrylic spray, both of which are available at art and craft supply stores. Or use clear nail polish. Cover the entire top of the decoration and base with the sealer. Be sure to cover the sides and top of every piece of wood. Apply several coats of the sealer. Let each coat dry thoroughly before you apply the next coat.

Sealing isn't necessary if you draw your own decorations. Draw pictures or designs right onto a thick cardboard base. An oval base can be turned into a colorful egg. A square or rectangular base can carry a message, such as "Remember Your Diet."

Now you are ready to attach the magnetized tape, which is sold in craft shops and some hardware stores. The tape can be cut with scissors. One side of the tape has a sticky surface, so that it can easily be attached to wood, paper, and other surfaces.

Cut two pieces of tape that are just a little shorter than the width of your base. Peel off the protective covering from the sticky side of the tape, and attach the pieces to the back of each base.

Finished? Take your magnets into the kitchen . . . and stick 'em up!

ANIMAL FATHERS

Many young animals need the care and protection of their mothers. And many need their fathers, too. There are animal fathers that build nests for their young, feed them, defend them, and carry them around. And some animal fathers rear their families entirely by themselves.

FEATHERED FATHERS

Most birds are devoted parents. They have to be because their young could never survive on their own. Usually, the male and female work together as they raise their young.

A bird's nest may be built by the female, the male, or both. Woodpeckers take turns as they chop out nesting holes with their chisel-shaped beaks. The male clings to a tree with his sharply curved claws. He braces himself with his stiff tail and starts drilling. After a while, the female takes over. They switch back and forth. The rat-tat-tat-

A father woodpecker feeds his hungry chicks. Later, it will be the mother woodpecker's turn to hunt for food.

tat of their drilling may last for days before their tree-hole nest is ready.

When the hole is deep enough, the female squeezes through the entrance. She lays four to six white eggs on a bed of woodchips. Then both parents take turns sitting on the eggs.

After the chicks hatch, the parents take turns babysitting. One parent stays in the nest while the other hunts for insects and grubs to feed the hungry chicks.

Woodpeckers always announce their arrival when they return from a hunting trip. As the father lands by the nest, he drums loudly on the tree trunk. He waves his head back and forth in front of the nest entrance. Then he hops to one side. The mother climbs out and flies off to take her turn hunting. The father squeezes in and stuffs the food he has brought into the chicks' gaping mouths. Now he's the one to stay home.

In about two weeks, the young woodpeckers are big enough to poke their heads outside the nest. When they are four weeks old, they begin to fly. For a few days they are fed by their parents outside the nest. Finally, they fly off for good.

Some nests are built by the male bird alone. A house wren does all the construction work himself, and he isn't satisfied with just one nest. When the mating season begins, he starts work on several.

He looks for likely holes and stuffs them with twigs and sticks. Any hole with a small opening will attract his attention. A small birdhouse in a garden is perfect. He may also build in an abandoned woodpeckers' nest, a hole in a wall, or the inside of a mailbox. One house wren built a nest in the pocket of a scarecrow's overalls.

A house wren may begin as many as six or seven nests, stuffing each of them with sticks and twigs. Usually he puts most of his effort into just two or three of these nests. When they are ready, he starts singing to attract a female.

When a female shows up, he leads her on an inspection tour. She pokes her head into each nest and picks out the one that appeals to her. She puts the finishing touches on the nest by lining it with feathers or grass. Then she lays five or six spotted eggs. She sits on the eggs herself while the male brings her food.

Both parents feed the newly hatched chicks. From dawn to dusk they fly back and forth, bringing insects to their young. Every few minutes, a parent arrives at the nest with another mouthful of food. The chicks may gulp down as many as 200 meals a day.

The young house wrens leave the nest in about two weeks, and their parents continue to feed them for two weeks more. When they are a month old, they fly away. But the father's work isn't done. He immediately cleans out the old nest and starts building new ones. He may help raise two or even three broods in a single summer.

No birds rear their young under more trying conditions than emperor penguins. They live at the bottom of the world, in the frozen wastes of Antarctica. Their home is a vast sheet of ice. Emperor penguins can't build nests, since trees, plants, pebbles, and even mud are not available. Instead, the males use their *feet* as nests.

In May, as the long Antarctic winter begins, each female lays just one egg. Right away, the male rolls the egg toward him. He places it on top of his webbed feet, where it is covered and kept warm by a feathered flap of skin that hangs down from his belly. From then on, he stands shoulder to shoulder in a huge crowd of father penguins. Each male has one egg balanced on top of his feet.

Antarctica's winters are fierce. Temperatures may drop to –70°F (–57°C). Winds of hurricane force howl across the ice. Day after frozen day, the father penguins guard their eggs. During this time they can't eat. There is no food for miles around.

After two months, the eggs begin to hatch. Each chick huddles between its father's feet, beneath the feathery warmth of his sagging belly. Every so often, the father bends down to feed his chick. The baby sticks its head into its father's mouth and gurgles a milky liquid from his throat.

Meanwhile, the mother penguins are miles away, swimming in the sea at the edge of the ice. They grow fat eating fish and squid. They finally come marching home when the young have hatched. The fathers are lean,

A baby emperor penguin huddles between its father's feet, beneath the soft, feathery warmth of his belly.

hungry, and tired. At last the mothers take over. Each female finds her mate and meets her chick for the first time. She slides in beside the male and takes the chick onto her feet. She then warms the chick and feeds it with food stored in her gullet.

Now it's the fathers' turn to eat and get fat. Together, the males waddle off across the ice. They head for the sea, where they will have their first meal in months. They return after a few weeks, and the fathers and mothers take turns caring for the chicks for about six months.

FURRY FATHERS

In the wild, a baby mammal can't survive without its mother. Its first food is always a rich diet of mother's milk. The word "mammal" comes from the Latin word *mamma,* which means "breast."

Many female mammals raise their young by themselves. Others live in family groups that include both parents. Sometimes the father plays an important role in family life.

No animal is a more tender and conscientious father than a male wolf. A wolf pack is like a big family. It is made up of the mother and father, their growing pups, and often some uncles and aunts.

The pups are born in the spring. At first they stay with their mother in her underground den, nursing and sleeping. Their father sleeps outside the den with the other wolves. All the wolves guard the den entrance. When they go hunting at night, they carry home food for the mother wolf.

When the pups are about two weeks old, their father visits them for the first time. He crawls into the den, sniffs the pups, and licks their fur. He may lie on his back and let them climb all over him.

After a month, the pups are romping and playing outside. Their father chases them, wrestles with them, and nips them gently. He never picks them up, however. Only the mother does that. If a pup wanders away, she lifts it by the scruff of the neck and carries it back to the den. The father may run alongside, whining to the pup and licking its face.

When the pups are ready to eat meat, all the wolves bring food home to them. After two months, the pups are big enough to leave their den for good. From then on, they live in the open with their mother, their father, and the rest of the pack.

Beavers live in family groups made up of the mother, the father, and their last two litters of kits. Often the whole family can be heard churring and chattering inside their lodge, which rises like an island of sticks from the middle of the beaver pond.

Every spring a new litter arrives. Just before the mother gives birth, the father moves out of the lodge and sets up bachelor quarters nearby. The older kits may move out with him, since the expectant mother can be very testy and nervous. When her new kits are two or three weeks old, the rest of the family returns home.

Beavers sleep during the day. At dusk they leave their lodge to feed on bark, twigs, and plants along the shores of their pond. The young kits follow their parents on their nightly rounds. They wait for the adults to cut down branches or twigs, then move in to share the meal. Often the whole family will crowd around a log to gnaw at the bark.

Both parents guard the kits. At any sign of danger, the adults slap the water or ground with their flat tails. When the kits hear that sound, they race for the pond, dive underwater, and swim back to the safety of the family lodge.

Baby monkeys are usually raised by their mothers, but marmosets have a different arrangement. Baby marmosets are cared for mainly by their fathers. These small monkeys live in the rain forests of South America. They leap and scurry through the trees, calling back and forth with shrill, birdlike voices.

A mother marmoset usually gives birth to twins. As each infant is born, the father takes it from the mother and cleans its fur. For the next six or seven weeks, he carries the babies on his back as the troop of marmosets moves swiftly through the forest.

A mother beaver nurses her little kits, as the father sits contentedly nearby. They all live together in a lodge that rises like an island of sticks from the middle of the beaver pond.

The infants cling tightly to their father's fur with tiny hands and feet. He hands the babies to the mother only at feeding time. When they finish nursing, he takes them back again.

When the youngsters are big enough to eat solid food, their father finds fruit and insects for them. He chews the food himself before giving it to them, since their baby teeth are just coming out.

In a few weeks, the youngsters are big enough to ride on their father's shoulders. Soon they make their first efforts to climb trees. If they stumble or fall, their father comes to their rescue. After four months, the young marmosets can race through the trees like experts. But they still cling to their parents' fur when they are frightened, and they sleep with them in the treetops at night.

FROG FATHERS

Most cold-blooded animals never see their offspring. As a rule, the female lays large numbers of eggs and leaves them to hatch on their own. But some reptiles, frogs, and fish do care for their young. Often it is the father who takes on the family responsibilities.

In the tropics, certain male frogs build nests for their tadpoles. The little South American smith frog constructs a nest of mud at the edge of a pond. He crawls into the water and turns in a circle until he has made a hole in the mud. Using his snout as a shovel, he pushes up mud along the sides of the hole and builds a circular wall. Then he pats down the mud with his front legs. Inside the mud wall is a pool of water several inches deep.

The smith frog sits in this pool and calls loudly for a mate. When a female comes along, she lays her eggs inside the pool. Both parents guard the eggs until they hatch. Then the tadpoles swim about in their private nursery, protected from enemies in the rest of the pond. When they change from tadpoles into frogs, they climb over the mud wall and hop away.

Arrow-poison frogs carry their tadpoles on their backs as they hop about through South American jungles. These frogs are brightly colored—a warning to other animals that they have poisonous skins. Indians catch them and smear their poison on the tips of arrows.

After a female arrow-poison frog lays her eggs, the newly hatched tadpoles wriggle onto their father's sticky back. For several weeks, he is a walking nursery, until the babies can swim on their own.

A female arrow-poison frog lays her eggs on the ground. Then the male stands by and guards the eggs. When the tadpoles hatch, they wriggle onto their father's sticky back and hang on with their tiny sucker-like mouths. For several weeks the father is a walking nursery. He may carry as many as 35 tadpoles on his back.

From time to time he dunks the tadpoles in a pool or puddle to keep their skins moist. They cling tightly to his back, since they are not yet strong enough to swim. One day, as their father jumps into a pool, the tadpoles drop off his back and swim away.

One South American frog carries living tadpoles inside his body. Darwin's frog is about the size of a cricket and lives in the forests of Chile and Argentina. It was discovered a century ago by the scientist Charles Darwin. You can imagine Darwin's surprise when he saw little froglets jumping out of a male frog's mouth.

When the female Darwin frog lays her eggs, several males crowd around to guard them. Just before the eggs hatch, the tadpoles inside begin to squirm. As the jelly-covered eggs quiver and shake, each male leaps forward and snaps up several eggs with his tongue. The eggs slide through a slit in the floor of his mouth and drop into a large pouch inside his body. This elastic pouch stretches from the male's throat all the way down to his hips.

Tucked safely away in the father's body, the eggs hatch. As the tadpoles grow, the male's body begins to swell and bulge. Gradually the tadpoles lose their tails and change into tiny froglets. When they are ready to leave their moist dark nursery, they jump one by one out of the male frog's mouth.

FISH FATHERS

Quite a few male fish guard their eggs and newly hatched young. One of the best-known is the little stickleback, which lives in ponds and streams throughout North America and Europe. Male sticklebacks build nests that are more elaborate than those of many birds. They collect bits and pieces of water plants, squirt them with a sticky fluid that comes from their kidneys, and glue them together.

A three-spined stickleback shapes his underwater nest into a long, neat pile. Then he pushes his way through the middle of the pile, forming a tunnel with a front and back entrance and a stream of water running through it.

When a female swims by, the male performs a zig-zag courtship dance and leads her to his nest. She squeezes into the tunnel, lays her eggs, and swims away. After the nest has been filled with eggs from several females, the male guards the eggs himself. He will attack any fish that comes too close. With his tail and fins, he fans fresh water through the tunnel. And he repairs any parts of the nest that break off and float away.

After the eggs hatch, the nest becomes a nursery for the little fry. For a few more days, the father stickleback continues to guard his family. If a baby stickleback wanders away, the father swims after it, takes it in his mouth, and carries it home.

Sea catfishes are called "mouthbrooders." Instead of building a nest, the male catfish uses his mouth as a nursery. He sucks the eggs into his mouth right after the female releases them into the water. For several weeks he swims about with a bulging mouthful of eggs the size of marbles. During this time, he can't eat.

When the eggs hatch, the babies remain in their father's mouth for several more weeks. Each newly hatched catfish has some yolk from its egg attached to its belly. It gets the food it needs from its yolk sac. But the father still can't eat.

When the young catfish are a couple of inches long, they are ready to swim off on their own. By now, the father's parental instincts are fading fast. If the young fish don't swim away at the right time, they might be swallowed by their hungry father.

One animal father, the seahorse, actually gives birth to his young. A male seahorse has a special brood pouch on his belly. When the female is ready to release her eggs, a small tube comes out of her body. She pushes this tube through an opening in the male's pouch. Then she squirts her eggs into the pouch, turns around, and swims away.

Inside the waterproof pouch, the eggs split open and the embryos start to grow. As they get bigger, their father's pouch swells like a balloon.

In about six weeks, the babies are ready to be born. Their father coils his tail around a strand of seaweed. He begins to twist and bend, trying to squeeze the babies out. Each time he tightens the muscles in his pouch, a little seahorse shoots into the water.

He may give birth to as many as 200 infants before his pouch is empty. They swim off in all directions. When the last one leaves the pouch, the father's belly is flat and his offspring have scattered into the sea.

RUSSELL FREEDMAN
Author, *Getting Born*

The male seahorse actually gives birth to his young. He has a special brood pouch on his belly, which swells like a balloon when it is filled with the growing embryos.

TWO-FOR-ONE PLANTS

How would you like to have a two-for-one machine? Put a candy bar into the machine, and out come two candy bars. Or perhaps you'd like to put in a dollar bill, a bicycle, or a guitar and get back two of each. Of course there is no such thing as a two-for-one machine. But there's something very much like it if you enjoy having plants in your home.

You probably know that most plants make more plants (reproduce) by means of seeds. The flowers of the plant produce seeds, and the seeds, in turn, produce new plants. But you may be surprised to learn that many of the plants you have at home or see for sale didn't come from seeds. Instead, they were grown from the leaves, stems, or roots of older plants. Producing new plants without using flowers or seeds is called vegetative reproduction. You can use this method to produce as many plants as you like.

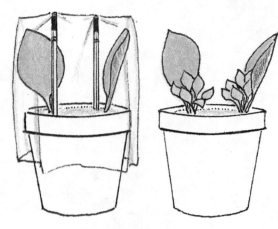

Leaf Cuttings

LEAF CUTTINGS

One easy way to use vegetative reproduction is to make leaf cuttings. African violets, gloxinias, and other soft-stemmed plants give good results with this method.

You will need the plant, a teaspoon, one flowerpot 5 inches (12 centimeters) in diameter, and several flowerpots 4 inches (10 centimeters) in diameter. You will also need a razor blade or a small, sharp knife, a transparent plastic bag, some short pencils, enough coarse sand to fill the larger pots, and enough potting soil to fill the smaller pots. (Don't use sand from the beach—it may contain salt.)

Fill the larger pot with the coarse sand.

Gloxinia

Stem Cuttings

Select a medium-sized leaf in good condition, and cut it cleanly from the plant, leaving a few inches of stem attached to the leaf.

Push a pencil down into the sand, making a hole deep enough to hold about half the length of the leaf stem. Insert the leaf, and gently press the sand to firm it around the leaf stem. You may put several leaves in the pot, but be sure that the leaves are at least 2 inches (5 centimeters) apart. Water the sand.

Unlike the parent plant, the leaf cuttings have no roots to absorb water from the sand. They will grow their own roots in time, but now you must protect them from drying out. To do this, make a moisture tent for them by propping up a transparent plastic bag on pencils or short sticks. The pot should be placed in good light, but never in direct sunlight. Water the sand only if it seems to be dry.

You will need to be patient. In three or four weeks, watch for tiny new leaves forming at the base of each cutting. When these leaves have grown to ½ inch (1 centimeter) in length, remove the plastic bag. Water the sand, and let the pot drain for an hour or more. Use the potting soil to fill as many of the smaller pots as you have new plants.

Now you must work very carefully to avoid injury to the roots of the new plants. Using the teaspoon, dig under a new plant, picking it up along with a clump of sand. Cut away or gently pull away the old leaf cutting that you started with, and plant the young plant, still within the clump of sand, in the potting soil. When you have finished with all the young plants, they will be able to live on their own.

STEM CUTTINGS

Another kind of cutting is the stem cutting. This method works well with plants that

Geranium

have fairly firm stems, such as geraniums. If you have a large, healthy plant, you can make several cuttings from it without injuring the plant.

First, fill a flowerpot 4 inches in diameter with potting soil. Press a pencil down into the soil to make a hole 2 inches deep. Now you are ready to choose a stem for cutting.

The best stems are from a part of the plant that is neither too old and woody nor too young and soft. The cutting should have three or four nodes—the places where leaves are attached. Cut the stem at an angle, using a sharp knife to get a clean cut. Remove all the flowers and buds and the lowest leaves from the cut stem.

Set the stem into the hole, and firm the soil around it gently. Water the soil and set up a plastic moisture tent, as with the leaf cuttings. Watch for new growth in the cuttings. A few days after you find new growth, remove the tent. Now you have a new plant.

Many people use a chemical called a rooting hormone to get faster results. The hormone may be bought at garden centers.

RUNNERS

Spider plants and strawberry geraniums (also called strawberry begonias) form new plants in still another way. The baby plants are formed on long stems, or runners, that grow from the old plant.

To get more plants, simply place pots of soil near the parent plant. Place a baby plant, still on its runner, in each pot. Pin the plants in place with bent paper clips. Don't move any of the pots. When you see that the baby

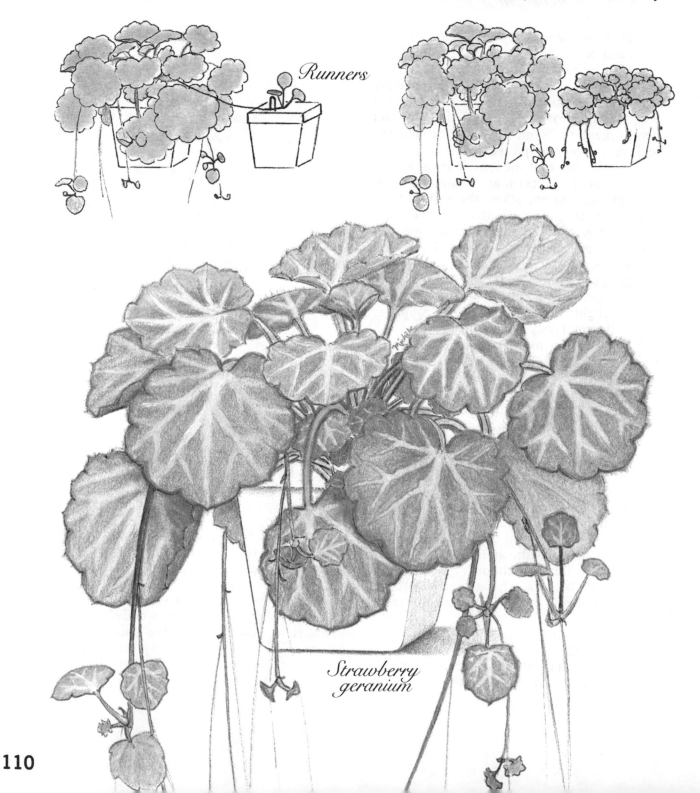

Runners

Strawberry geranium

110

Division

African violet

plants are growing well, cut the runners, and you will have a fine new set of young plants. You can do this over and over again, with both the old plant and the new ones.

DIVISION

Plants such as African violets and some kinds of ferns and ivies can reproduce by a method called division. Examine your plant carefully. You may find that a second plant is growing alongside the old plant. The new plant is usually smaller, but it is complete with roots, stems, and leaves. It can be divided, or separated, from the older plant and allowed to grow independently.

First, water the plant lightly, and lift or knock it out of the pot. You may be able to pull the plants apart, even though the roots are entangled. If you cannot pull the plants apart, cut through the roots so that each plant gets a fair share of them. (Remember that a big plant needs more roots than a small one.) You cannot avoid damaging some of the roots. But if you replant each division promptly in its own pot and water it well, you will usually end up with more plants than you had to begin with. It's like having a two-for-one machine!

LEO SCHNEIDER
Author, *You and Your Cells*

111

MUMMERS ON PARADE

They come trooping down the avenue in a blaze of fabulous color, glitter and gold, feathers and frills. Some of the marchers look like fugitives from a zany Halloween masquerade party, while others have the appearance of creatures from a space fantasy. Many wear winglike backpieces that make them look like gaily plumed birds.

String bands, led by platoons of banjo players, swing and sway as they plunk out such old favorites as "Happy Days Are Here Again" and "My Old Kentucky Home." Clowns cavort, marchers strut, and everywhere there is fun and frolic. For this is the Mummers' Parade, held in Philadelphia every New Year's Day and an annual tradition for more than 80 years.

Probably few among the hundreds of thousands who line the parade route along Philadelphia's Broad Street are aware that the once-a-year extravaganza is an outgrowth of the mummers' plays that were a popular form of entertainment in Europe several centuries ago.

What went on then, however, was a far cry from today's Mummers' Parade. The original mummers were English country folk who put on simple plays at Christmastime and passed around the hat for whatever small change was offered. Performers wore costumes and masks, and the word "mummer" is believed to come from the German word *mumme* (which means disguise or mask).

The most popular of the English mummers' plays was based on the legend of St. George. In that version, St. George, the English knight, is challenged to a duel by a Turkish knight. While the two knights fight it out, other mummers perform a sword dance with mock weapons made of wood. One of the knights is killed and then brought back to life by a doctor. It is believed that the play symbolized the death of the earth in winter and its rebirth in spring.

First performed in England in the 1600's, mummers' plays spread to Scotland, Wales, and Ireland. The plays were performed throughout Britain until the middle of the 1800's. And, although the tradition has faded, groups of mummers—wearing overalls covered with shredded newspaper—can still be seen in England today.

The mumming tradition was brought to the United States in colonial days by early European settlers. At Christmastime, English colonists put on disguises when visiting neighbors. German settlers decked themselves out as clowns, and the Swedes and Finns made merry by rhythmically banging pots and pans—an early form of mummers' bands.

In Philadelphia, this type of mummery evolved into formal clubs, first organized in the 1840's. During the holiday season, costumed members of the clubs would parade through the streets of their neighborhoods.

On New Year's Day in 1881, a Philadelphia newspaper reported that bands of costumed paraders made the streets "almost like a masked ball."

Around the turn of the century, the clubs began adding string bands. These had such colorful names as Mixed Pickles, Dark Lanterns, and Golden Slippers. The first full-scale Mummers' Parade was held in 1901. As the bands paraded through the streets, they accepted gifts of cakes from friendly neighbors and local bakeries. A cake-cutting ball marked the climax of the festivities.

Today there are 53 marching clubs, with some 23,000 members. There are string band clubs and comic clubs. And there are fancy clubs and fancy brigades—which wear the gaudiest outfits, like the ones shown here. In the early days, members made their own costumes, but now the more elaborate outfits are professionally tailored. And instead of cakes, the clubs now compete for $300,000 in prize money.

People from all walks of life are in the clubs—dock workers, clerks, accountants, policemen. Several generations of one family may march together in one club—or may compete against each other by belonging to different clubs. Most of the marchers are men and boys, but a few women and girls can be found scattered among them.

Mummers rehearse all year long. And as soon as one parade ends, planning for the next one begins. What draws these people together is the fun and excitement of the big parade—that magical moment when the bands and fancy brigades step off down Broad Street in an explosion of color. The music builds to a crescendo, the crowds cheer, and the mummers do their strut—bending one knee, then the other, swaying from side to side.

That's when the blood surges, the pulse quickens, and the long hours of rehearsal seem worthwhile. As one 10-year-old mummer put it: "Being in the parade is a fun feeling. When I hear the music, I get goose bumps."

POPULAR CRAFTS

One of the exciting things about crafts is that there are so many different ones to try. Everyone can find at least one special one to become good at. But where do all the ideas for these craft projects come from? Many craftspeople are inspired by nature. They think about how they can express what they see with materials they enjoy working with. And many craftspeople like to work with recycled materials, to protect nature. Do you like nature and working with "bits and pieces"? If you do, perhaps you might want to create a basket of flowers.

A BASKET OF FLOWERS

Making a basket of flowers from leftover scraps is a great way to add a charming hanging to your room. You will need a brown paper bag, a bit of lace, a large piece of cardboard, and pieces of colorful felt.

First cut the paper bag into 30 narrow strips. Take 15 of the strips and arrange them side by side on a piece of the cardboard. Glue down only the top edges of the strips. Weave the remaining strips to form a basket-weave pattern. Glue the bottoms in place, and cut out a basket shape.

From the cardboard, cut out a basket handle and a half circle that will serve as the background for the flowers. Glue the handle and the flower background to the basket.

Cut out flowers and leaves from the pieces of felt. Make a pretty arrangement as you glue them onto the background. You can add sequins and yarn pompoms for an extra touch. Cover the handle with lace, and outline the basket with colorful felt.

Now you have an all-season basket of flowers for hanging.

FABRIC DOLLS

Some people think that making dolls is even more fun than playing with them. You can make a cuddly fabric doll with some un-

Making a colorful basket of flowers from leftover scraps is a fun way to add a charming hanging to your room.

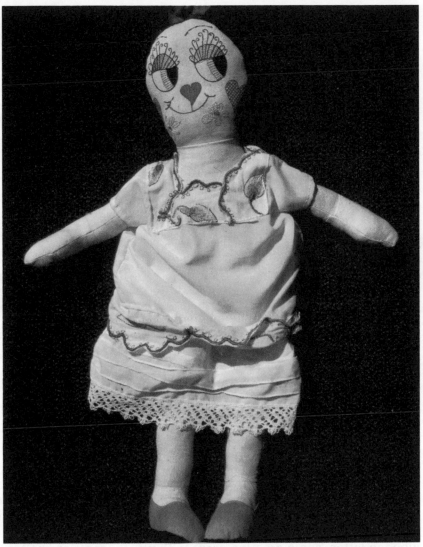

Cuddly fabric dolls can be anything you want them to be. You can make them out of any kind of fabric and in any size and shape.

bleached muslin that is cut from a pattern and then stuffed with fiberfill. Your doll will come to life with a few extra touches—an embroidered hearts-and-flowers face, pink felt slippers, and a red bow for her head. Making doll clothes is fun, too. Use your imagination. A scrap of lace can become a petticoat. Or you can dress her in some of your old baby clothes.

Fabric dolls can be anything you want them to be. You can make them out of any kind of fabric and in any size or shape. Try making a doll that looks like you or one of your friends.

WINDOW KITES

Capture the colors of your favorite season with tissue-paper window kites. These kites are for decorating rather than for flying.

Start with a package of brightly colored tissue papers and some thin wooden dowels. (You'll need four for each kite.) Using string, tie the dowels together to form a square frame.

Mix and match the tissue papers until you find a color combination that appeals to you. Then cut the papers into strips. Glue the strips together, allowing the same amount of overlap between each strip. You should end up with a multi-colored piece of tissue paper that is slightly larger than the frame.

Lay the paper under the frame, and arrange it so that there is an even margin all around. Glue the margin onto the frame. When the glue has dried, trim any overhanging edges. Then attach a string loop to one corner of the kite and hang it in a window. Hang two kites together to make a mobile.

Tissue-paper window kites are for decorating, not flying.

Use paper cutouts to make whimsical wooden letters.

WHIMSICAL WOODEN LETTERS

Cut-paper decorations have been used for centuries on furniture, glass, ceramics, and wood. Try using paper cutouts to make a whimsical wooden letter. You will need a wooden letter, some greeting cards with pictures, a tube of hobby silicone, and varnish. (Silicone is used to add a three-dimensional effect as well as to affix the pictures to the letter. Read the instructions on the tube. Silicone must be carefully handled.)

Paint or stain the wooden letter, or leave it its natural color. Then select pictures that will fit its size and shape. Carefully cut out the pictures and arrange them on the letter. You can dampen your cutouts to curve and shape them in a realistic way.

For a three-dimensional effect, work in this way: Start with the background cutouts, and attach them to the wooden letter with silicone. Next, add the middle ground cutouts. Add enough silicone to the backs of these pictures to make them stand out from the background. The more silicone you use, the more the pictures will stand out. The foreground pictures are added last. You will probably want to use extra silicone to make these pictures stand out the most.

After the letter is completely decorated and the silicone has dried, paint the finished piece with a clear varnish. Two or three light coats are better than one heavy coat.

STAINED GLASS

Stained glass is colored glass that has been cut into pieces and then arranged to form a design. The pieces of glass are held together by thin strips of lead. Stained glass is especially beautiful when light passes through it. For this reason, it has been used for centuries to make beautiful church windows.

Today, people also work with stained glass to create various kinds of decorative objects. An example of an attractive and at the same time useful item is a stained-glass plant hanger that can be hung on the wall. Since light will not be shining through the plant hanger, opalescent glass, rather than clear glass, is used. This kind of glass contains rich streaks and swirls of color. And if mirrored glass is also used, your plant will be reflected, creating an illusion of depth.

LANDSCAPE PICTURES

Try "painting with fabric"—sew a landscape. Begin by making a simple outline drawing of your favorite landscape scene. It's difficult to show small details with fabric. So draw large shapes—trees, mountains, hills, rivers. Be sure to have a main point of interest, such as a house or a barn.

Transfer your designs onto colored pieces of fabric. Cut out the fabric, leaving a small margin of material all the way around. Carefully turn the margins under and press with a hot iron. Then sew the fabric by hand directly onto a piece of canvas that has been stretched over and stapled onto a wooden frame. As you sew, stuff the pieces with cotton batting to create a three-dimensional effect for your landscape. You can add details to the landscape by embroidering branches, birds, and flowers with contrasting colors of thread.

WENDIE R. BLANCHARD
Managing Editor
Creative Crafts magazine

A stained-glass plant hanger is both beautiful and useful.

If you love nature and working with fabrics, you can sew a landscape.

JASPER THE GIANT

Once upon a time, giants were very important. Just about every town and village had one. Naturally, the bigger the giant was, the more important he was. When a town had a really big giant, people came from all over the kingdom to see how big he truly was. And while they were in town, they bought postcards with the giant's picture on them to send to the folks back home. A town with a very large giant could sell enough postcards during the tourist season to pay for food and firewood for the rest of the year.

Now, the town of Brinkendorf had a really giant-size giant named George. Brinkendorf was the envy of all its neighbors, for George sold more postcards than any other giant in the kingdom.

One year, however, George announced that he wanted to retire.

The mayor was immediately alarmed. "Retire? What about our tourist season?"

"I have that all figured out, Mr. Mayor," said George. "I've written to my nephew Jasper. He told me he'd be happy to take my place as the Brinkendorf Giant."

"Well, I don't want to give you a swelled head, George," said the mayor, "but you *are* a pretty spectacular giant. If we are to let you retire, your replacement must also be spectacular."

"Don't worry," replied George. "Jasper has all the qualifications." And he proceeded to tell the mayor how Jasper's mother and father had been unmistakable giants, and how his grandfather Homer was such a gigantic giant, he could easily have become an ogre, had he set his mind to it.

It was enough to convince the mayor. The town council voted George a handsome pension, and sent off a telegram to Jasper, offering him the position of Brinkendorf Giant.

When Jasper wired his acceptance, the mayor's wife began to plan a "welcome-the-

118

new-giant'' party. Everyone in Brinkendorf helped in the preparations. They hung bunting on all the shop fronts. Banners floated from every pole. The Brinkendorf Brass Band polished up its tubas and practiced its triumphal marches.

Jasper had written that he would arrive on Tuesday at noon. So on Tuesday, just before noon, the townspeople assembled in the town square, ready to give him a proper giant-sized welcome.

The clock in the town hall struck twelve. The townspeople were all gathered in the town square. The mayor cleared his throat. The mayor's wife straightened his tie. The bandleader rapped with his baton.

Suddenly a fellow came whistling around the corner and approached the mayor. "Pardon me, sir," the fellow began.

"Not now," said the mayor. "We're expecting our new giant."

"I think you're expecting me," said the fellow.

"Nonsense," said the mayor, looking the fellow up and down. "Now, if you don't mind . . .''

"My name is Jasper," the fellow said.

The mayor's jaw dropped. The bandleader's baton clattered onto the music stand. The tuba player's big brass horn thudded to the ground.

The mayor's wife was the first to regain her tongue. "*You're* Jasper?" she croaked. "But you're . . . short!"

"Nonetheless," said Jasper, "I'm your new giant. My mother was a giant, and my father was a giant. That makes *me* a giant."

"Now, see here, young man," declared the mayor, "this job calls for a, er, *large* person."

"*You* see here, Mr. Mayor," said Jasper. "You offered me a job, and I accepted. Nothing was said about how tall I would be."

Jasper was right, of course. The town had offered him the job, and they had to honor their contract.

"But I'm sure you can see, young man," said the mayor, "that you're not qualified for the giant opening. We do, however, need someone to sell postcards, and you would do fine for that job."

So it was agreed that Jasper should take the postcard-salesman position, and the mayor advertised for another giant. Pretty soon a really gigantic giant was hired. His name was Jerome, and he was about twice as tall as the church.

Jerome was put to work posing for postcard pictures with his arm around the clock tower, and sitting on the post office. The mayor clicked his shutter until there was only one picture left on his roll of film.

"Here, Billy," he said to his son, "take my picture with Jerome."

Billy took the camera and looked through the viewfinder at the mayor, who had climbed up on Jerome's knee. But, although he could see his father, all he could see of Jerome was a knee. So he began backing up to get as much of the giant as he could into the picture.

Suddenly Billy took one step backward too many! He backed right into the town well, lost his balance and fell—*splash*—right into it!

"Help!" cried Billy from the bottom of the well.

"Oh, dear!" cried the mayor's wife.

"Do something, Jerome!" cried the mayor.

Jerome stepped up to the well and tried to put his huge fist into it, but his hand was much too big.

The mayor's wife had hysterics. The mayor dithered. The giant sulked. But Jasper acted.

Quietly and efficiently he lowered the bucket down into the well. "Grab hold, Billy," he called.

Soon Billy was out of the well and drying his mother's tears.

When the tourist season started, a strange thing began to happen. The story about how Jasper had rescued Billy began to get around. Soon more and more tourists were asking Jasper to sign autographs and wanting to have their pictures taken with the postcard salesman. Pretty soon, everyone was ignoring the Brinkendorf Giant. Jerome got his nose out of joint and quit.

"I'm sorry, Mr. Mayor," said Jasper. "I certainly didn't mean for this to happen."

"That's all right, my boy," mused the mayor, who was a pretty enterprising fellow. "I have an idea for a brand-new tourist attraction for Brinkendorf."

"What's that, sir?" inquired Jasper.

"You, my boy!" answered the mayor. "You may be a short giant, but you're a giant-size hero. Now step back there, just in front of the well. I have some new postcard pictures to take . . ."

INDEX

ILLUSTRATION CREDITS AND ACKNOWLEDGMENTS

15-Artwork adapted from the
18 April-May issue of *National Wildlife* magazine, © 1973 National Wildlife Foundation
20 Courtesy Cleveland Health Museum
22 Cyndy Waters—The 1982 World's Fair
23 ©Al Stephenson—Liaison
25 Wally McNamee— *Newsweek*
26 Artist, Michèle McLean
28 Larry Stevens
29 Keith Gunnar—Bruce Coleman
31 Mario Ruiz
32 Activision; Activision; Mattel Electronics; Activision; Mario Ruiz
33 ©Michael Grecco—Picture Group
34 Peter D. Capen; Peter D. Capen; Jeff Foott
35 Jeff Foott
40 "The Parasol Vendor" from *Merchants of the Mysterious East* © 1981 John Lim. Published by Tundra Books
41 The Mansell Collection; The British Museum
42 The Mansell Collection; BBC Hulton Picture Library; The Mansell Collection
43 The National Gallery, London
44 The Metropolitan Museum of Art, Gift of the New York State Historical Society, 1979; The Bettmann Archive
45 Illustration by Mary Shepard ©1934 (renewed 1962) by P. L. Travers. Reproduced from *Mary Poppins* and *Mary Poppins Comes Back* by P. L. Travers. By permission of

Harcourt Brace Jovanovich, Inc.
46-©Akira Uchiyama—Photo
47 Researchers
48 Courtesy William Tricker
49 Courtesy Van Ness Water Gardens; ©A. Wambler—Photo Researchers; W. H. Hodge—©Peter Arnold
50 Courtesy Slocum Water Gardens
51 Pamela J. Harper
52-Jenny Tesar
53
54 ©Gordon Gahan—Photo Researchers
55 Arie de Zanger
57 Bil Baird's Marionettes
62-©Kjell B. Sandved
63
64 Dale Jorgenson—Tom Stack & Associates; ©Steve Firebaugh—Bruce Coleman
65 Kleeman—Tom Stack & Associates; ©Russ Kinne—Photo Researchers
66 ©Lynn Karlin; The Bettmann Archive; Mary Evans Picture Library
67 Mary Evans Picture Library
68 ©Lynn Karlin
69 Concord Free Public Library
70 The Bettmann Archive
72-Line illustrations by Ernest
73 H. Shepard. Copyright in the United States 1928 by E. P. Dutton and Co. Inc. Copyright renewal ©1956 by A. A. Milne. Copyright under Berne convention. Coloring of the illustrations ©1974 by Ernest H. Shepard and Methuen Children's Books Ltd. Reproduced by permission of Curtis Brown Ltd., London

74-Artist, Dale Barsamian
75
76-Courtesy of Scholastic
79 Photography Awards, conducted by Scholastic Magazines, Inc. and sponsored by Eastman Kodak Company
84-Artist, Michèle McLean
88
94 J. Albertson—Stock, Boston
95 Martha Swope © 1982
96 Poem from *Old Possum's Book of Practical Cats*, copyright 1939 by T. S. Eliot; renewed 1967 by Esme Valerie Eliot. Reprinted by permission of Harcourt Brace Jovanovich, Inc.; illustration by Rudyard Kipling ("The Cat That Walked by Himself"); Jane Howard
97 Jane Howard
98 Courtesy the Paper Bag Players
100-Jenny Tesar
101
102 Ted Levin—Animals Animals
103 Suinot—The Image Bank
104 Jen and Des Bartlett—Bruce Coleman
106 Edward S. Ross
107 Jen and Des Bartlett—Bruce Coleman
108-Artist, Michèle McLean
111
112-John McGrail
113
114 Courtesy Katie Richardson
115-Courtesy *Creative Crafts*
117 magazine